The Legislative Journey of Employment Discrimination

Ermira Babamusta, Ph.D.

NY ELITE PRESS

The Legislative Journey of Employment Discrimination
Copyright © 2020 Ermira Babamusta, Ph.D.

ISBN: 978-1-7349354-2-4 (paperback)
ISBN: 978-1-7349354-3-1 (Ebook)

Library of Congress Control Number: 2020908355

Ebook Available at:
www.nyelitepress.com

NY Elite Press
New York, NY

For more information or to contact the author please go to:
www.facebook.com/ErmiraBabamustafans

Because of the dynamic nature of the Internet, any web addresses or links contained in this book may have changed since publication and may no longer be valid.

Book Cover & Design: Charlyn Designs
Author Photo: Olsi Beçi

First publication May 2005/Master's Thesis, Minnesota State University, USA

Other Publications:

Political Trust in Kosovo
ISBN: 978-1-7349354-0-0 (paperback)
ISBN: 978-1-7349354-1-7 (Ebook)

Diplomacy and Nation Building in Kosovo
ISBN: 978-1-7349354-4-8 (paperback)
ISBN: 978-1-7349354-5-5 (Ebook)

TABLE OF CONTENTS

LIST OF FIGURES

LIST OF TABLES

ABSTRACT

The purpose of this study is to discover the relationship between legislative and judicial decisions and employment discrimination charges. The study raises the following research question, "To what extent do government actions influence employment discrimination?" The hypothesis is that government interference has a major effect on the volume of employment discrimination charges filed.

The research study includes detailed qualitative data formulated in a timeline to assess the nature of influence of legislative and judicial decisions on employment discrimination. In addition, statistical data are included to test the progress of employment discrimination from 1992–2004.

The results indicate that government actions and Supreme Court decisions have essential roles in the growth of employment discrimination charges filed. More specifically, the regression analysis demonstrated that ADA has had a major effect on the volume of disability discrimination charges, after the law was implemented in 1994. There was a significant difference in the number of age discrimination charges. 29 U.S.C. 621 had a major effect in decreasing charges of age discrimination. Furthermore, substantial changes were seen in racial and sex discrimination charges.

ACKNOWLEDGEMENTS

I am grateful for my family and sister for their continued love and support. I am truly blessed to have them in my life.

Personal gratitude is extended to Research Advisor Dr. Scott Granberg-Rademacker, who helped plan, organize, and proofread the study through several versions of the document, to Dr. Doran N. Hunter, chair of MSU Political Science/ Law Enforcement, for his tremendous help and exceptional support, and to professor of the Urban and Regional Studies Institute, Dr. Perry Wood for contributing his time and assistance.

I am grateful to professor Dr. Jackie Vieceli for helping in proofreading and for her substantive moral support throughout, and whose contribution helped make this study possible.

Personal gratitude is also extended to the Honorable Congressman Mark Kennedy, former Representative of Minnesota's Sixth Congressional District, and his staff for the wonderful support and for the role they played in assisting with the study. I was blessed to be part of Congressman Kennedy's team, which I am eternally grateful, while pursuing my graduate studies in Political Science. This opportunity gave me a front row seat at the inner workings of diplomacy at the legislative government branch. I have a deeper appreciation for the American leadership and our great American nation.

Special appreciation is extended to the extraordinary staff of Congressman Kennedy for giving me a remarkable Capitol Hill experience during the summer of 2005: Patrick Shortridge, Chief of Staff; Elisa Aglieco, Executive Assistant; Ed Skala, Legislative Director; Anne Mason, Press Secretary; Emily Jungwirth, Legislative Assistant; Timothy Morrison, Legislative Assistant; Matt Skaret, Legislative Correspondent and Michael Yost, Legislative Correspondent. I want to thank all the staffers for being friendly and welcoming because they made my Washington D.C. experience a memorable one.

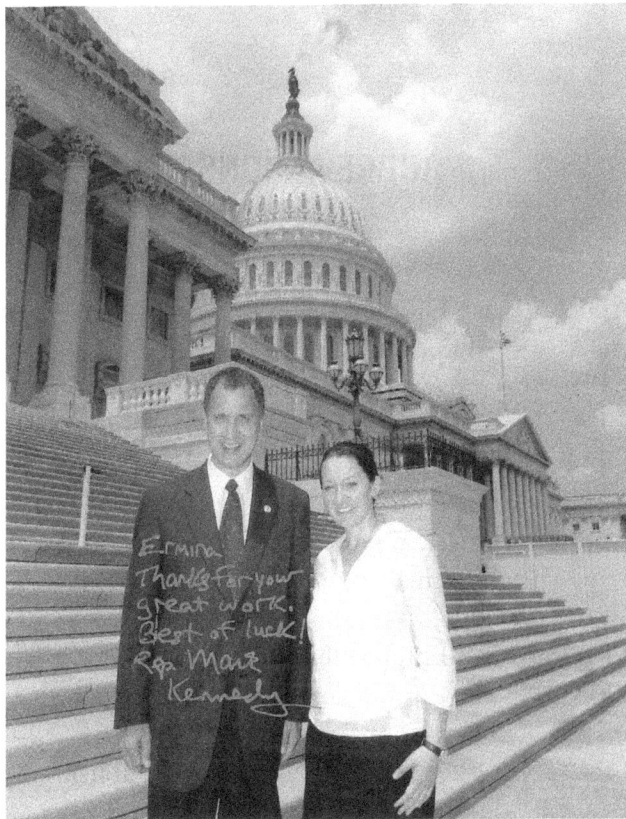

Congressman Mark Kennedy and Ermira,
U.S. Congress, DC (2005)

ABBREVIATIONS

ADEA	Age Discrimination in Employment Act
ADA	Americans with Disability Act
CFR	Congress Federal Register
CRA	Civil Rights Act
DDA	The Disability Discrimination Act
EEO	Equal Employment Opportunity
EEOC	Equal Employment Opportunity Commission
EPA	Equal Pay Act
FEB	Fair Employment Board
FEPC	The Fair Employment Practice Committee
NLRB	The National Labor Relations Board
OFCC	Office of Federal Contract Compliance
PCGEP	President's Committee on Government Employment Policy
PDA	Pregnancy Discrimination Act
RFRA	Religious Freedom Restoration Act
Title VII	Title VII of Civil Rights Act
U.S.C.	U.S. Federal Code

Chapter 1
INTRODUCTION

"Of my two "handicaps," being female put many more obstacles in my path than being black."
Shirley Chisholm

Today's workplace portrays a different picture than the one that Shirley Chisholm, the first African American woman elected in Congress in 1968, described in the 60's. We expect to see a workplace where employees take legal measures against employment discrimination to promote equal employment opportunity for all individuals. Whereas in the 50's and 60's employment opportunity was limited on the basis of race and gender (Ospina & O'Sullivan, 2003).

Since then, the government and the Supreme Court have taken actions to prohibit employment discrimination. For instance, Congress created the Equal Employment Opportunity Commission (EEOC) in 1964 to prohibit discrimination in the workplace. EEOC implemented numerous statutes including Title VII of the Civil Rights Act (Title VII), Equal Pay Act of 1963 (EPA), Civil Rights Act of 1991 (CRA), Age Discrimination in Employment Act of 1967 (ADEA), Titles I and V of the Americans with Disabilities Act of 1990 (ADA) and Rehabilitation Act of 1973. The United States Constitution (the Fifth and Fourteenth Amendments) and federal agencies created by Congress have given additional protection to employees in cases of discrimination. In addition, Supreme Court decisions have influenced policy to weaken employment discrimination (Wood, 1990).

This book focuses on employment discrimination and explores the effectiveness of anti-discrimination laws and policies formulated by the government. The focal question of this study is, "To what extent do government actions influence employment discrimination?" It is crucial to understand the relationship between legislative laws and employment discrimination in order to study changes and trends in employment discrimination practices. The issue is very complex. One of the main reasons is that it is extremely difficult to apply the same laws that prohibit discrimination in all discrimination cases, due to the variety of Supreme Court's interpretation of the laws. Because of the variations, it is unclear what to expect. More important, there is a lack of empirical evidence to test the connection between the laws and the trends in employment discrimination.

There are several forms of employment discrimination. In general, employment discrimination means any unlawful treatment towards an employee on the basis of race, gender, religion, national origin, sexual orientation, equal pay, disability, and age. Typically, an employer must prevent employment discrimination and must forbid discriminatory practices in the workplace under Title VII, including bias in hiring, termination, promotion, compensation, and other practices (Title VII, 703 (a) (1), Civil Rights Act of 1964).

If sexual harassment occurs, or any unwelcome behavior that constitutes sexual favors in the workplace or pregnancy-based unfairness happens, these conditions create a hostile work environment that fosters discrimination (Bradford, 1990). This form of employment discrimination is known as discrimination on the basis of sex. In *Henson v. City of Dundee* (1982), the court ruled that favoritism based on granting sexual favors when it creates a hostile work environment violates Title VII. In these situations, women or men are seen as "sexual playthings" thus creating a hostile workforce environment that is demeaning to the employees (EEOC, 1995).

On the other hand, the concept of employment discrimination, particularly on the basis of sex is very complex and has created controversy and inconsistency in government actions. Should a woman applicant inform the employer about her pregnancy status? Does an employer violate the law by dismissing a pregnant woman when the pregnancy prevents the employee from performing the job? Does an employer commit unlawful practices when excluding fertile women from jobs in a workplace that is exposed to lead?

In the case of *International Union, United Automobile, Aerospace & Agricultural Implement Workers of America, UAW v. Johnson Controls, Inc.,* (1991) the Supreme Court overruled the decision of the Seventh Circuit (in *United Auto Workers v. Johnsons Controls,* 1989) maintaining the exclusion policy of all pregnant women with the intent of protecting the pregnant women and their unborn children from exposure to lead.

The Supreme Court grounded its ruling in the Pregnancy Discrimination Act (PDA) which implies that pregnant or "potentially pregnant" women should be treated the same as others "who are similar in their ability or inability to work" (EEOC, 1995). The interpretation of the language in this case contradicts the previous rulings, and therefore, makes the concept of employment discrimination very complex and creates controversy.

Fuentes (1972) argued that Title VII and EPA excluded employment discrimination of teachers, unlike the Executive Order 11478. Therefore, "women's groups have focused on the Office of Federal Contract Compliance (OFCC) in filing charges of discrimination against educational institutions" (p. 17). More important, the rulings of EEOC and the courts under Title VII, established principles, which are implemented by agencies at the federal and state levels. Fuentes (1972) concluded that courts faced difficulty in establishing discrimination on the basis of the individual. This further adds controversy to the debate over employment discrimination.

Generally, the body of law provides protection to victims of discrimination. EEOC has responded to the violation of law and has followed a process of conciliation and litigation to resolve discrimination issues (Wood, 1990). On the contrary, ending employment discrimination has created implications and controversy. Prior to 1972, "EEOC was able to resolve favorably for complaints only about 6% of all discrimination charges" (Wood, 1990, p. 507).

In addition, statutory interpretations and judicial findings have created controversy over the role of the Supreme Court in employment discrimination law (Rutherglen, 1995). This has increased the controversy on the issue. For instance, in *Chevron U.S.A., Inc. v. Natural Resources Defense Council, Inc.* (1984), the Supreme Court concluded that the agency's interpretations are reasonable, however in *Sutton v. United Air Lines* (1997), the lower courts narrowed the interpretation of the definition of disability. Furthermore, the courts refused deferral to EEOC. This demonstrates inconsistency in the Court's decisions. In addition, since Title VII and ADA were further amended, perhaps the influence of the legislative laws on age discrimination practices will not be clear and positive.

On the contrary, Rutherglen (1995) argued that employment discrimination law and the Supreme Court have proven to be effective. "Mainly by expanding the scope of statutory prohibitions against discrimination through the theory of disparate impact" and other means including disparate treatment, burden of proof and burden of persuasion to prove intentional, direct, and indirect discrimination (Rutherglen, 1995). However, the challenge that the government faces today is the role and the nature of influence on discrimination practices.

In the past, there have been few attempts at testing the connection between legal theory and factual information (Connell, 1991; Paetzold and O'Leary-Kelly, 1996; Knapp and Kustis, 1996), employment status and discrimination (Fuentes, 1972; Smith, 1980; Chambers and Goldstein, 1986; Weinberg, 1996; Manni, 2003; Pynes, 2004). For example, Winberg's studies focused on women's profession and discrimination cases. Knapp and Kustis (1996) attempted to estimate the total possible costs of sexual harassment. Paetzold and O'Leary-Kelly (1996) explored the impact of Supreme Court decisions on hostile workplace environments. Smith (1980) examined the relationship of labor and discrimination practices.

However, the studies are very limited and cannot be applied on a broader scope of employment discrimination. The general notion is that government action impacts the number of employment discrimination charges filed. However, this argument has gone largely untested. The central goal of this book is to shed some light on the controversy of employment discrimination and answer the important question of the efficacy of influence of government actions.

Chapter 2 concentrates on the scope of governmental response to discrimination practices and summarizes familiar controversies regarding the Supreme Court's interpretation of law. The literature review examines these topics and offers insight and comments with regard to issues identified by leading scholars. It is the intent of this study to direct attention to the performance of government and the Supreme Court and the nature of influence in employment discrimination. To answer the central research question, relevant laws, executive orders, and court decisions are identified and synthesized into a complete discussion timeline from 1986 to 2005. In the course of constructing the timeline, the historical background of EEOC and the Law are examined, with specific attention to executive orders, federal agency guidelines, and Equal Opportunity Employment landmark cases.

Chapter 3 operationalizes employment discrimination in a way that can be examined empirically in a model to test the effects of relevant laws, executive orders, and court decisions. In addition, the empirical data incorporates control variables accounting for social, geographical, political, and demographic variation into the model, so that the desired effects can be isolated. Numerical data were collected from EEOC studies and the U.S. Census Bureau to formulate an econometric modeling technique including time-series, descriptive statistics, and regression analysis to answer the central research question. Individual variables are theoretically constructed from relevant cases and laws.

The *dependent variable* includes disability, equal pay, pregnancy, gender, sexual harassment, national origin, race, and religion discrimination. The *independent variable* consists of landmark cases and government actions as they relate to the dependent variable. This approach tests the implicit though systematically untested assumption that many have about employment discrimination laws, cases, and executive orders—that they make a tangible difference. Several hypotheses are crafted to test the effect of major cases, laws, and executive orders on employment discrimination. These effects are then measured using regression analysis and other econometric methods.

The following chapter summarizes the findings of the research. Figures from Table 11 suggest that there is a connection between government actions and the number of filed employment discrimination charges. For example, the Disability Discrimination Act of 1995 (DDA) accounts for the decrease of filed cases regarding employment discrimination on the basis of disability. The Supreme Court's decision in *Harris v. Forklift Systems, Inc.,* (1993) accounts for the increase of sexual harassment charges filed. Chapter 5 offers comments regarding the future of employment discrimination.

Chapter 2
LITERATURE REVIEW

Over the past 30 years, researchers (Hays and Kerney, 2003; Kellough, 1992; Weinberg, 1996; Smith, 1980; Rosenthal, 1973) have demonstrated that employment discrimination based on race, sex, religion, national origin, physical disability, and age has a long and painful history. The general assumption is that actions taken by the government (laws, court cases, and executive orders) have an immediate and definite impact on curbing employment discrimination. However, this contention has gone largely untested. Just how far the impact extends, however, has been a matter of some controversy.

Researchers agree (Seldon, 2003; Rutherglen, 1995; Morris, 1995; Fuentes, 1972; Doyle, 1997) that any dispute over employment opportunity is best understood by examining the plight of historically disadvantaged groups who have suffered because of race, ethnicity, gender, age, disability, equal pay, national origin, religion, sexual orientation, and other traits or circumstances. Nonetheless, the same scholars have been unable to agree on questions relating to the scope of governmental response to instances of discrimination, as well as the use of legal language by legislators and the courts.

2.1 Scope of Governmental Response to Instances of Discrimination

Despite the struggle for equal employment opportunity, the equal protection laws, and the merit system created to ensure that applicants are selected on the basis of their abilities, discrimination was very common especially in the public sector. Hays and Kearney (2003) point out, for example, that William Howard Taft initiated a policy of segregation of whites and African Americans within the Census Bureau. Fewer African American workers were appointed in the South because whites opposed their employment.

In his article, Kellough (2003, 210) emphasized that racial discrimination was encouraged during the administration of Woodrow Wilson, with the segregation of offices, rest rooms, and lunchrooms. In addition, "a fitness test for federal employees" required the applicants to include a photograph— thereby providing yet another avenue for gender and race discrimination in hiring practices. While it is possible that bias in hiring, promoting, terminating, and other types of harassment would occur due to the segregation practices; Pynes (2004a) argued that workplace harassment imposes substantial costs that lead to loss of productivity, lowering of morale, and loss of reputation of the employers.

In addition, employment discrimination is likely to lower public confidence in public institutions, bureaucratic agencies, and the public services that each provide. Indeed, discrimination could produce a worst-case scenario which "would divide the country along racial lines" resulting in violence, social unrest, and disruption in military discipline (Kellough 2003, 210). Although, the test requirement did not carry through, it was obvious that the color of one's skin was a key factor, in particular, in the federal sector.

It was not until the 1940's that the federal government responded to employment discrimination. Early action began under the Roosevelt administration and "the most egregious discriminatory practices were first confronted by the federal government" (Kellough, 2003, p. 210). The administration feared that demonstrations in Washington D.C. would quickly spread across the country and focus attention in racial division in the United States. Therefore, the Roosevelt Administration deemed it to be important for the government to step in to prevent civil upheaval in society.

Despite Roosevelt's actions to prevent discriminatory practices, little was done to implement the law. For example, Roosevelt issued Executive Order 8587, which prohibited racial discrimination in the federal sector (Federal Register, 1940). However, Kellough argued that despite the president's efforts in the 1940s to prohibit racial discrimination, unfair employment practices remained. "But, as little was done to enforce the act or the order," concluded Kellough, "the policy of nondiscrimination was more a sentiment than a reality" (Kellough, 1992, 121).

African Americans, who made up 9.8 percent of the U.S. population in 1940, only held 4.2 percent of the jobs in the federal sector, nearly all in the lowest positions. As research showed, government acts did little in reducing employment discrimination (Kellough, 1992) though this was not for lack of issue saliency. In fact, the Roosevelt administration took action in an attempt to reduce discrimination by signing Executive Order 8802 just one week before an anti-discrimination protest was planned in Washington. The country was becoming more aware and enraged about discriminatory employment practices and demanded the government's attention in enforcing fair employment policies.

The aim of Executive Order 8802, signed in 1941, was to open doors for new programs designed to protect the interest of previously disadvantaged groups. This order essentially banned the federal government and federal contractors from discriminating on the basis of race, color, or national origin (Federal Register, 1941). For the first time, presidential efforts started the enforcement of fair employment practices. The effort of the Roosevelt Administration is further demonstrated by the establishment of the Federal Employment Practice Committee (FEPC), which for a short time acted as an advisory committee created by executive order under contract compliance authority.

Graham (1992) argued that Roosevelt's fair employment committee "added to defense contractors a new social provision that required contractors to protect the civil rights of minorities" (p. 53). However, since most of the key seats in the Congress favored segregation, FEPC had little support. Thus, funding came from the Executive Office of the President. Roosevelt's efforts demonstrated attempts to fight racial discrimination in the labor force.

Afterward, Presidents Truman and Eisenhower established committees, under executive orders, in efforts to bring minorities into the work force. In fact, President Truman appointed his own advisory committee, the Fair Employment Board (FEB) within the Civil Service Commission, to keep watch over job discrimination by government agencies and contractors (Graham, 1992, p. 53).

In 1955 Eisenhower eliminated the FEB and created a new committee, called the President's Committee on Government Employment Policy (PCGEP). The PCGEP was independent of the Civil Service Commission and was set up as an agency-funded entity so that direct appropriation from Congress was not needed.

Despite the presidential efforts for civil rights legislation, Congress was unwilling to cooperate. This is not to say that President Kennedy was discouraged from continuing the fight to protect the minority's rights. Kennedy took a different approach from the previous presidents. He issued Executive Order 10925 in 1961, which was signed at a White House Ceremony, to avoid confrontation with an uncooperative Congress. In addition, Graham (1992) suggested that for the first time, "the executive order was linked to affirmative action"[1] (Graham, 1992, p. 54).

As understood by the Kennedy and Johnson Administrations, the order meant that government employers and contractors would have to place extensive efforts in recruiting minorities. The selection process was based on the merit criteria (Graham, 1992, p. 54). This is a very important step to equal opportunity for all employers, because employees selected the best person for the job, not taking into consideration race, gender, or other reasons. Graham (1992) concluded that Kennedy's executive order was a significant and influential action in the federal government, because affirmative action ensured that employees would be treated fairly without consideration of their race, creed, color or national origin.

The extent to which government action influences discrimination may depend on the approach of the leaders. President Kennedy and President Johnson took aggressive approaches by

---

[1] Affirmative Action was used in the Wagner Act of 1935, which gave the National Labor Relations Board (NLRB), the authority to level out unfair job practices. See Graham (1992, p. 54) for details.

attempting to control discrimination practices. President Johnson expanded the ban on employment discrimination to all government contractors. As a response to the congressional opposition, he transferred EEO's responsibility to the Civil Service Commission, via Executive Order 11246 (Kellough, 1992, p. 123).

According to the study of minority group employment in the federal sector conducted by the U.S. Civil Service Commission (1965), during Kennedy's administration, "blacks slightly exceeded proportional representation in the federal service, holding 13.1 percent of federal jobs in 1963"; thereby suggesting that African Americans were gradually being integrated into the federal services.

Perhaps the best evidence that government action has had an impact in employment discrimination practices is found in the change of the government's focus. The focus changed from concerns to recruiting minorities to integrating them into middle and higher levels of the federal services. The shift translated from recruiting minorities in the federal sector, to increasing minority representation in higher positions and in higher bureaucracy (Kellough, 1992, p. 123).

Furthermore, concerns began to focus on prohibiting discrimination on the basis of gender, which gave women protection in federal jobs. Weinberg (1996) concluded that a major change came as a result of President Johnson's Executive Order 11375 issued on October 13, 1967. The order prohibited discrimination on the basis of gender, and the public employers were forced to take heed, or risk losing their federal funding (Weinberg, 1996, p. 325). This had a dramatic effect on how funds and fellowships were distributed among departments and offices within institutions of higher education.

Weinberg (1996) argued that as a result of the executive order, colleges and universities insisted on fairer internal procedures, such as allocating fellowship funds on the basis of merit and evaluating female candidates fairly. The effectiveness of the order extended to equal treatment for women and minority groups.

For the first time women were placed under the federal EEO program, due to the enforcement of Executive Order 11375. EEOC examined federal employment patterns between 1970 and 1990, to assess the process of integrating women and minorities into middle and higher levels of the federal government. Data on the representation of women and minorities revealed that integration to higher-level positions was gradual and incremental, though it was unclear how much of the increase was due to affirmative action.

The study of Minority Group Employment in the federal government (1990), reported that female employment in the middle and higher grades increased after 1971. For example, female employment increased to 1.25 percent per year from 1972–1984, compared to an average rate of 0.54 percent from 1968–1971. In grades 13–18, female employment gained an average annual increase of

0.83 percent from 0.34 percent prior, and black employment increased at an average rate of 0.21 percent per year in 1981 compared to 0.13 percent per year in 1978. The study showed that an increase occurred in the employment rate of women in middle and higher-level positions. This is another example that demonstrates that government efforts were geared toward protecting women and minorities.

The suggestion that the implementation of the executive orders and government actions restrained discrimination has created much controversy. Bernard Anderson (1996, p. 301) indicated that, "enforcement strategies should be measured by the degree to which they help achieve [the] goal." Although the Department of Labor provided enforcement guidance, contracting agencies varied widely in their enforcement practices (Anderson, 1996, p. 299). This controversy culminated with the increase of the number of staff and departments in the contracting agencies that devoted little time, effort, staff, and energy to the affirmative-action requirement (Anderson, 1999). This explains that transformation occurred during enforcement practices.

As a result of President Johnson's Executive Order 11246 in 1978, contracting-agency enforcement personnel (personnel assigned to enforce affirmative action policies on contract agencies) were reassigned to the Labor Department, in a new agency called the Office of Federal Contract Compliance (OFCC). New leadership in 1981 in OFCC may have caused the controversy to be noticed. Furthermore, during President Carter's administration, the Equal Employment Opportunity Commission (EEOC) issued guidelines for the federal program, placing great emphasis on numerical goals and timetables in agency affirmative action plans, but during the Reagan years, EEOC backed away from that approach (Kellough, 2003).

During the Reagan administration OFCC employees assigned to conduct compliance reviews throughout the U.S. were "neither committed to the organization nor to affirmative action" (Anderson, 1996, p. 299). More important, Reagan's failed efforts to withdraw the Executive Order 11246 attracted wide criticism on enforcement practices. In other words, if the political leadership fails, the goals will go unfulfilled. In this case, the staff of the OFCC had little confidence in the agency and had no intention to carry out its mission in regards to implementing the enforcement practices.

Despite the increase in enforcement practices through the early 1990's, both the OFCC and the Department of Labor "focused on voluntary compliance rather than strong enforcement as the preferred strategy for implementing the Executive Order" (Anderson, 1996, p. 300). The impact of Executive Order 11246 has been affected dramatically by the strategies and available resources for enforcement. It would be critical for the government to take new initiatives in prioritizing enforcement activities.

On the contrary, a second shift of government focus occurred in 1993, during the new administration of President Bill Clinton. President Clinton brought new changes in enforcement practices by redefining the goals of the administration, and by implementing new alternatives that called for successful outcomes. The following monograph provides a sampling of the type of changes the Clinton Administration focused on:

> "With the inauguration of the new administration in 1993, the emphasis of OFCC was shifted back to a high priority on enforcement. A new enforcement initiative was adopted, with a goal toward (a) focusing on the worst offenders; (b) targeting the most obvious areas of noncompliance; (c) strengthening the sanctions applied for noncompliance; and (d) settling disputes quickly and effectively.
>
> The backlog of OFCC discrimination cases, some more than 15 years old, was eliminated. One especially notable case, involving the Honeywell Corporation, was settled with $16 million in back pay and penalties for 1,200 women who

> had been denied employment
> in previously all-male jobs."
> (Anderson, 1996, p. 300)

Anderson concluded that a serious effort was made to revise the OFCC regulations in order to reduce paperwork, to reorganize the enforcement process, and to expand training for OFCC staff (Anderson, 1999, p. 300). This action demonstrated the great efforts of the government to expand minority and female employment and to increase their opportunities in the management and executive jobs.

On October 20, 2004, President George W. Bush signed Executive Order 13360, entitled "Providing Opportunities for Service-Disabled Veteran Businesses," which increased federal contracting and subcontracting opportunities for service-disabled veteran businesses. This further adds to the government efforts to promote equal opportunity for all workers. In an interview for this study with the Honorable Congressman Mark Kennedy, who represented Minnesota's Sixth Congressional District, stated that:

> "Each individual in our society
> should have the same chance
> to succeed in our booming
> workforce. There has been a great
> deal of attention paid to this issue
> for a long time now, and I'm

pleased that my daughters will
have the same chance for thriving
careers as my sons." (Interview,
2005)

The government is committed, devoted and
determined to achieve equal job opportunity and fair
employment practices.

2.2 Implications of the Supreme Court's interpretation of the Law

There is considerable evidence to suggest that the
interpretation of employment discrimination laws is
a practice riddled with uncertainty (Rosenthal, 1973;
Smith, 1980; Bryner, 1981). This section examines
and analyzes that evidence. In addition, the Court's
general interpretation of employment discrimination,
as well as an examination of various landmark cases
in discriminatory practices will be presented.

One of the earlier and most controversial
examples concerned the role and involvement of the
legal system. Smith (1980) suggested that fighting
employment discrimination "has been a concern of
social policy for almost four decades, but a consensus
on the role of the legal system should play in the
quest for equal employment opportunity has not
yet evolved" (Smith, 1980, p. 493). In other words,
the debate focused on the role of the legal system in

interpreting laws and legislation concerning equal employment opportunity cases.

Furthermore, Smith (1980) believed that the enforcement of employment discrimination policies has resulted in "overlapping and conflicting regulations, inconsistent results and general confusion" (p. 493). Smith may simply have been referring to the early failed attempts of the Presidential executive orders, which in some cases were not enforced effectively. However, the civil rights movement of the 1960s generated new regulations (i.e. Title VII of the Civil Rights Act of 1964) that reinforced the prevention of unlawful practices.

Other examples revolve around the language found in the law used by the courts to identify the classification of employment discrimination. For instance, to establish that an unlawful practice had occurred, the Equal Employment Opportunity Commission (EEOC) "had to make findings as to the presence or absence of '*reasonable cause*' to make its own rulings" (Rosenthal, 1973, p. 92). This meant that the burden of proof was placed heavily on the discriminated individuals, who must show sufficient evidence to justify the unlawful practices, for their claims to fall under reasonable cause.

According to EEOC, reasonable cause is determined if "the discrimination occurred based upon evidence obtained in investigation. Some reasonable cause findings are resolved through negotiated settlements, withdrawals with benefits, and other types of resolutions, which are not characterized as either successful or unsuccessful conciliations" (EEOC, 1998). In this case, only after a full investigation takes place can the EEOC determine reasonable cause for discrimination has likely occurred.

However, this is rather difficult because it means showing sufficient evidence to prove discrimination. In *Griggs v. Duke Power* (1971), the role of the Supreme Court focused on determining the criteria used in employment discrimination. In this case, the Court examined where the burden of proof lies with the employer.

Due to the inconsistencies among the Court rulings, Congressional regulations and policies of regulatory agencies, the Court has faced problems in its decisions (Bryner, 1981). For instance, in the cases of *Teamsters v. United States* and *TWA v. Hardison*, the Court interpreted the legislative history of Title VII, and construed it to justify a broad variety of different views, without considering legislative intent. For example, the majority and dissenting opinion in *Teamsters v. United States* & *TWA v. Hardison* address legislative intent. However, the views of the justices are different, thus resulting in two different opinions. This shows the implications and problems of interpreting the language of the law in regards to discriminations instances.

Another problem is directly related to the Court's inconsistency with the EEOC guidelines. For instance, in early decisions such as *Griggs v. Duke Power* the Court gave great deference to

EEOC guidelines, but in later cases such as *General Electric v. Gilbert*, the Court's decisions contradicted those guidelines that were "inconsistent with earlier commission guidelines, and were in any event, entitled to only *some* consideration in the Courts decision" (Bryner, 1981, p. 425). The inconsistencies in Court findings create problems and contradictions that make it harder for the employee to know his/her rights about filing.

These problems are related to the lack of clarity regarding the regulations of employment discrimination. Despite the good intentions of lawmakers, there is still no clear definition of discrimination, especially when it comes to employer practices. Thus, agencies define discrimination depending on the work environment and socioeconomic factors (Bryner, 1981). This leads to various interpretations of the policies, depending on the employer.

In his article, Bryner looks at how Congress, the Courts and public agencies have interpreted laws of employment discrimination differently. "Until 1978, more than twenty agencies besides the Equal Employment Opportunity Commission were responsible for administering employment discrimination laws (Bryner, 1981, p. 416). Carter's Reorganization Plan of 1978 sought to curb employment discrimination, however, the courts, EEOC and the Office of Federal Compliance Programs shared responsibility to implement the discrimination laws and take the necessary measures if the employer breached the rules (Bryner, 1981).

Bryner summarizes important variables and factors that have contributed to the controversy of equal employment opportunity policy. The author demonstrates that public agencies have used a variety of equal employment policies. Agencies try to avoid violating the laws; therefore, the actions that agencies take vary according to the organization. For example, federal agencies and contractors refer to EEOC and OFCC guidelines for specific employer practices in regards to affirmative action and industry wide practices.

However, when considering general societal practices, statutes for veterans and handicapped and all protected groups in the federal sector are considered instead of the EEOC guidelines. Even though EEOC provides protection against the three major types of discriminatory practices (discriminatory intent, disparate treatment, and disparate impact). Since there is a lack of a clear definition of employment discrimination and general guidelines of identifying discrimination in the workplace, agencies take actions depending on industry-wide discrimination, or the result of general, societal discrimination (Bryner, 1981, p. 427).

More important, the term employment discrimination is broad and leaves room for uncertainty and inconsistency. Courts have to identify the degree of discrimination necessary to establish if the unlawful practices are direct, indirect or intentional. However, these concepts are not as easy as they seem, indeed it has been argued that the concept of discrimination has never been clearly defined, nor have its limitations (Rutherglen, 1995, p. 123). This makes it difficult for agencies to apply the law according to the agency's practices and puts restraints on the role of the courts.

The majority opinion in *United States v. Weber*, was based on the purpose of Title VII, rather than on the literal wording of the law. However, Justice Brennan emphasized the narrowness of the ruling and argued that the undefined details of the law put a constraint on the literal reading of the law. He stated, "We need not define in detail the line of demarcation between permissible and impermissible affirmative action plans" (*United States v. Weber*). Therefore, courts struggle with interpreting employment discrimination laws.

In addition, the Court has been expected to be clear and consistent in developing policy guidelines but has been unable to do that. The Court has struggled with the interpretation of the laws and has relied instead on shaping its decisions around the specific features of each case (Rutherglen, 1995, p. 425). The uncertainty has limited the Court's potential consistency in interpreting laws.

Congress has delegated to the courts the authority to formulate and implement equal employment opportunity policy. EEOC has developed guidelines independently of Congress (Bryner, 1981, p. 426). However, as Bryner (1981) argued, the variety of controversy involving equal employment opportunity policy is "the fruits of congressional inaction, agency weakness, and judicial legislation" (p. 427).

For instance, the 1972 and 1978 amendments of Title VII, failed to address the unclarity of statutory provisions. Instead it extended the coverage of law and changed the enforcement procedure. EEOC was charged with implementing the statute and authorized to file judicial actions (Player, 1992, p. 13). The 1978 Amendment added a definition of "sex" that included "pregnancy and childbirth." Despite all this, Congress did not address equal employment opportunity efforts of the government as a whole (Bryner, 1981, p. 427).

Congress reacted to *Wards Cove Packing v. Antonio* (1989) and passed many amendments to the CRA of 1991, including banning discriminatory adjustment of test scores, allowing damages for intentional discrimination, and redefining the burdens in disparate impact cases (Player, 1992, p. 13).

CRA of 1991 further expanded Title VII, but it did not add any amendments to the Age Discrimination Employment Act of 1967. Section 4(f)(1) of ADEA included "language that significantly narrow[ed] its coverage by permitting any 'otherwise prohibited' action 'where the differentiation is based on reasonable factors other than age'" (Smith, 2005). Therefore, the interpretation of Title VII, prior to 1991 in *Wards Cove,* was exactly the same as the language in ADEA. However, ADEA allows for recovery of liquidated damages (Player, 1992). The complexity involved in the interpretation of the language demonstrated the need for clarification and changes of the law.

In 1965 when the Title VII debate was very heated, the addition of "age" as a protected class was proposed. At the beginning, this proposal was rejected. However, Congress's efforts to formulate legislation to stop age discrimination did not go in vain. Secretary of Labor directed by Congress issued the 1965 report that outlined the principles of ADEA. In 1978 its authority was transferred to EEOC. The 1974 amendment of ADEA extended coverage to governmental employers. Amendments in 1978 increased the protected age class from age 65 to age 70.

However, the amendments in 1986 removed the age 70 and up-age limit on protection. Amendments in 1990 clarified standards "by which employees could be granted severance pay as part of early retirement programs and established waiver of age discrimination claims" (Player, 1992, p. 15). The Amendment of 1991 made procedural changes in the ADEA. ADEA, while very similar to Title VII, offers standards and provisions that are specifically applicable to age discrimination cases. Its purpose is to prohibit discrimination on the basis of age and to provide guidance for employers who experience discriminatory practices in the workplace.

Furthermore, Title VII's "English-only rule," implemented by EEOC, allows restriction of communication in non-English languages only for nondiscriminatory reasons. In 2002 EEOC received 228 charges challenging this rule (EEOC, 2002). U.S. Census Bureau reported that in 1990, approximately 31.8 million Americans (13.8 percent of the population) spoke a language other than English in the home. Of those individuals, 6.7 million individuals (2.9 percent of the total population) spoke little or no English (U.S. Census Bureau, 1999). This creates communication difficulty and brings up the question, "What language should be used at the workforce?"

The EEOC adopted the guidelines on English-only rules, 29 C.F.R. § 1606.7. The guidelines state that English-only rules must be justified by "business necessity." Examples of business necessity include customer and employee communication or safety concerns in a hazardous situation (Personnel Policy Inc, 1994).

Title VII has caused great controversy in the debate of national origin discrimination. The Lower courts have struggled with the interpretation of Title VII regarding the English-only rules and the effectiveness of the EEOC guidelines. In *EEOC v. Synchro-Start Productions. Inc.*, 29 F. Supp. 2d 911, 914–15 (N.D. Ill. 1999) the court concluded that English-only rules may create discriminatory work environment based on national origin.

However, in *Roman v. Cornell Univ.*, 53 F. Supp. 2d 223, 237 (N.D.N.Y. 1999) the court justified adopting the English-only rule for business reasons to avoid interpersonal conflicts among workers, prevent misunderstandings between non-foreign language speaking persons and foreign language speaking individuals. In *Long v. First Union Corp.*, 894 F. Supp. 933, 941 (E.D. Va. 1995) the court ruled in favor of implementing the English-only rule and stated the rule is necessary and legitimate to prevent employees who intentionally want to use a foreign language to make non-foreign language persons feel left out.

In *Garcia v. Gloor*, 618 F.2d 264 (5th Cir. 1980), the lower court considered and justified the English-only rule due to business necessity (keeping harmony among ethnic groups in the workplace and avoiding leaving out any employees because of not speaking a foreign language). In this case, the company required the employees to speak English only during work hours, unless serving Spanish-speaking customers. Gloor was fired because according to the company, he violated the rule.

The court stated that the rule should be limited to bilingual employees during work hours, for the purpose of limiting ethnic tensions between workers and avoiding misunderstandings between customers and employees. After this decision, EEOC's created the national origin guidelines, stated in 29 C.F.R. 1606.7(c), which require the employer to create the appropriate procedures when the rule is not followed correctly.

However, in the second Garcia case, *Garcia v. Spun Steak Co.*, 998 F.2d 1480, 1489 (9th Cir. 1993) the court rejected the EEOC's English-only rules guidelines. In this case, the Spun Steak Company complained that some workers were using bilingualism with the intent to harass and humiliate other workers. Two Spanish employers, who were using offensive language with African American and Chinese American workers, filed discrimination charges.

According to the EEOC guidelines, the employees are required to speak English during work hours, but not including other times, such as lunch breaks. The Ninth Circuit Court of Appeals reasoned that Title VII does not protect employees who express their cultural identity. The court rejected the claims of the Spanish employees and found that the EEOC's guidelines on English-only rules "could not be applied to truly bilingual employees because such individuals do not suffer any adverse impact from these rules and holding that the guidelines impermissibly presume that English-only policies have a disparate impact without requiring proof of such" (EEOC, 2002, 48).

However, the court did not rule out the argument that the English-only rule can reduce tensions between employees of different ethnicity. Cruz (1995) suggested that the decision of the second *Garcia* questions the validity of the English-only rule, and its effectiveness should be determined on a case-by-case basis. The Supreme Court refused to hear the second *Garcia* case; therefore, it brings scrutiny to the national origin discrimination on the English-only rules. Therefore, employees are left without necessary guidance in such cases (Cruz, 1995).

Many researchers (Jones, 1993; Doyle, 1995; Collignon, 1997; White, 2000; Manni, 2003) have questioned the effectiveness of the Law. Doyle (1995) questioned the motives of DDA and called it a "disabling law" rather than an "enabling statute" (p. 78). He argued that DDA made some difference, however, it created more doubt due to the narrow definition of disability, and lack of a strategic enforcement agency. The Court's interpretation of the definition of disability "is troubling, particularly in the context of workplace discrimination" (White, 2000, p. 537). These uncertainties point out the ineffectiveness of the law and lack of a clear definition of terms.

The term "qualified individual with a disability" is defined as, "an individual with a disability who, with or without reasonable accommodation, can perform the essential functions of the employment position that such individual holds or desires" (42 U.S.C.§ 12111(8) (1994). Title I of the Americans with Disability Act (1990) states that:

> "No covered entity shall discriminate against a qualified individual with a disability because of the disability of such individual in regard to job application procedures, the hiring, advancement, or

discharge of employees, employee compensation, job training, and other terms, and privileges of employment." (42 U.S.C.§ 12112 (a) (1994)

Title I of ADA prohibits employers from discriminating against qualified individuals with disability in the workforce. Congress formulated the definition of an individual with disability as "a person who has a physical or mental impairment that substantially limits one or more major life activities" (ADA, I (501). However, ADA is a broadly worded statute (White, 2000) and very controversial.

ADA clearly defines employment discrimination, but it leaves an open question of what is considered a major life activity. How can one determine whether a person is substantially limited in a major life activity? Does it include mitigating measures such as medicines? What impairments are considered disabling? For example, if a person is a diabetic, but is on medication, would an employer be free to fire or not to fire the person because he/she was a diabetic? For instance, in *Sutton v. United Air Lines Inc.,* (1999) the twin sisters who suffered from myopia could correct the problem if they wore glasses. This demonstrates the complexity of the issue.

The Congress saw the lack of an enforcement agency, therefore, Congress delegated rulemaking authority to EEOC to implement the ADA's employment requirements (42 U.S. C. § 12116). EEOC formulated regulations, to comply with Congress, including an Interpretive Guidance that would specifically address the dilemma of the mitigating measures.[2] EEOC took the position that determining if a person is qualified as disabled *does not* include mitigating measures.

> "The determination of whether an individual is substantially limited in a major life activity must be made on a case by case basis, without regard to mitigating measures such as medicines, or assistive or prosthetic devices." (White, 2000, p. 535)

However, some lower courts rejected EEOC's position and others accepted it. In *Washington v. HCA Health Services of Texas Inc.,* (1998); *Arnold v. United Parcel Services Inc.,* (1998) the lower court ruled that mitigating measures generally *need not to* be taken into account; in *Sutton v. United Air Lines Inc.,* (1999) the court ruled that mitigating measures *need to* be taken into account; in *Matczak v. Frankford Candy and Chocolate Co.,* (1997) the decision was to assess impairment in unmitigated cases; and in

---

[2] 29 C.F.R. pt. 1630, app. § 1630. 2(j) (1999). The Interpretive Guidance was subject to the same notice just like the regulations.

Gilday v. Mecosta County (1997) it was concluded to take mitigating measures into account in some cases.

A number of circuit courts questioned the credibility of EEOC. In fact, in *Sutton* the Supreme Court refused to defer to the EEOC's views in determining the scope of ADA's protections. However, in *Chevron U.S.A., Inc., v. Natural Resources Defense Council, Inc.,* (1984), the Supreme Court ruled that courts defer to agency interpretation of statutes when the interpretations are reasonable and if the Congress has transferred authoritative power to the agency.

To address the interpretation problem the Courts used "a textualist approach to statutory interpretation that finds in the statute itself an answer to the interpretive question posed" (White, 2000, p. 536). However, whether to consider the "mitigating measures" posed by ADA added to the controversy, taking into consideration that the language of ADA is vague. It is likely that the Court's inconsistencies may demonstrate the Court's unwillingness to give up interpretive power to an administrative agency. This controversy takes away the focus from improving the lives of those who are disabled and providing them with their fundamental rights. Instead, the Court's rejection of EEOC's regulations has turned into a political implication.

2.3 The changing concept of employment discrimination

2.3.1 The Concept of Discrimination

Section 703 (a) (2) of Title VII defined discrimination as:

> (a) it shall be unlawful employment practice for an employer ....
>
> (b) to limit, segregate, or classify his employees or applicants for employment *in any way* which would deprive and *tend* to *deprive* any individual of employment opportunities or otherwise adversely affect his status as an employee, because of such individual's race, color, religion, sex, or national origin. (Civil Rights Act of 1964)

Title VII classified "unlawful employment practices" as discriminatory acts on the basis of different categories. Rutherglen (1995) referred to discrimination as "a process of noticing or marking a difference, often for evaluative purposes" (p. 127). According to Title VII, discrimination involved categorizing people into different groups according to race, color, religion, sex or national origin and giving them unfair treatment and unequal rights from other persons who are not part of the classified groups. *Griggs v. Duke Power Company*,[3] further strengthened the impact of the Civil Rights Act of 1964 in prohibiting employment discrimination. Chambers and Goldstein (1986) argued that "without *Griggs,* Title VII would have had little impact upon the historic problems of discrimination which it was intended to correct" (Chambers, Goldstein, 1986, p. 16).

Indeed, the census conducted by the Bureau of the Department of Commerce in 1983 revealed that 2.7 million African Americans were employed between 1972 and 1982, an increase of 1.4 million (Bureau of Census, 1983). Evidence such as this underscores the effectiveness of Title VII and its impact on prohibiting employment discrimination practices. However, the courts placed emphasis on requiring the showing of intent to discriminate.

2.3.2 The Scope of Discrimination

The Supreme Court considers two types of discrimination, disparate treatment and disparate impact to prove employment discrimination. Both factors add to the variations and the creativity of the Court's interpretation of the civil rights laws and the legislation concerning equal employment opportunity cases. Motivation proved by direct

---

[3] Refer to Table 7 for a complete overview of *Griggs v. Duke Power Company* case.

evidence and mixed motive has created a problem of proof for Courts in discrimination cases.

Direct Evidence

Spoken or written words against a protected class is considered as direct evidence of illegal motive in employment discrimination (Player, 1992). For example, the statement "If this were my company, I would not hire any blacks" clearly presents an expression of prejudice towards African Americans (EEOC v. Alton Packaging Corp, 11th Cir., 1990). The prejudice towards African Americans influenced the employer's decision in hiring individuals from this racial group. But, if such evidence is challenged, the employer must show that there is a link between his statements and the challenged decision (Player, 1992).

In *Griggs v. Duke Power Co.* (1971), the Court found that the test showed no direct link between the quality of work, the employees, and the production of the company. Direct Discrimination must show a direct relationship between the victim of the employment discrimination and the discrimination practices committed by the employer. For instance, a direct discrimination in an unlawful practice based on gender, must prove that the woman is treated less favorably than the man.

The issue of pregnancy in particular, has led to further complications. Bamforth (1993) raised the following question:

> "Does an employer commit an act of unlawful sex discrimination in dismissing a woman employee on learning that she is pregnant, when the pregnancy would prevent her from working at the time when the task for which she was specifically recruited fails to be performed?" (p. 56)

Bamforth (1993) concluded that, despite the fact that direct evidence pointed toward unfair treatment between men and women, it would be difficult for the courts to interpret the law when it would be almost impossible to assume circumstances when men are pregnant. In this case, to be considered direct discrimination, the victim must show that gender played a motivating part in employment decisions of the employer. However, it would be very difficult for the courts to consider the treatment based on gender. The courts must consider strong evidence in the direct discrimination cases, which makes it very hard for the judges to decide.

Single Motive Theory (Pretext)

Under Title VII, a plaintiff may file an employment discrimination claim under a single motive theory also referred to as the pretext motive (Spognardi, 2003). If the plaintiff establishes a prima facie case by showing initial inference of illegal motivation, and is successful, the burden falls on the employer to show justifiable nondiscriminatory reasons. "The employee then must show that that the reason was false and a pretext for illegal bias" (Spognardi, 2003). However, the burden of proof in a single motive theory case remains on the plaintiff to persuade the Court that the employer's reasons are not legitimate and are a pretext for discrimination.

Mixed Motives Theory

Mixed Motive theory requires the presence of legitimate and illegitimate motivation at the same time (Player, 1992). An employer may make employment decisions for various reasons, including legitimate and discriminatory reasons (Spognardi, 2003). The Civil Rights Act of 1991 added to the language of Title VII that a practice is considered discriminatory when established "when the complaining party demonstrates that race, color, religion, sex or national origin was a motivating factor for any employment practice, even though other factors also motivated the practice" (CRA, 1991). In other words, if the motivation shows discriminatory reasons, the practice is considered illegal, even if there are other legitimate reasons involved.

In *Price Waterhouse v. Hopkins* (S. Ct. 1989) a woman who was the senior manager filed a suit against the firm for violating Title VII, because of discrimination on the basis of sex. The plaintiff claimed that the defendant's sexual stereotyping and personality problems with other co-workers were the reasons for her denial of partnership in the firm.

The District Court found the firm liable, not on charges of intentional discrimination on the basis of gender, but because the firm had consciously maintained a system which, in this partner-candidacy decision "had given weight to biased criticisms without discouraging sexism or investigating comments to determine whether they were influenced by sexual stereotypes" (*Price*, 1989). The Court of Appeals concluded that the firm could avoid liability charges, only if it clearly presented evidence that proved that the firm would have taken the same decision even if discrimination had not played a role. This gives the firm the possibility to prove that the legitimate factors would have resulted in the same decision.

Another case, *Desert Palace, Inc., d/b/a Caesars Palace Hotel & Casino v. Costa*, (02 U.S. 679, 2003) caused a great controversy (Spognardi, 2003). In a 9–0 decision, the Supreme Court rejected the direct evidence requirement to prove discrimination. The Court ruled that circumstantial evidence is enough for the employee to win a mixed-motive theory case.

According to the Court's reasoning, even if other legitimate reasons existed, the employee could prove discrimination by presenting circumstantial evidence that the employer "relied in part on a discriminatory reason in making its decision" (Spognardi, 2003). This makes it easier for the employee to file discrimination charges and to win the case.

Disparate Treatment

The disparate-treatment theory requires evidence to prove the employer's subjective intent to discriminate. In the absence of direct evidence, discrimination can be proved through circumstantial evidence. However, this makes it more difficult to prove discrimination. The employee must show evidence necessary for a prima facie case, articulate a legitimate and nondiscriminatory response and show proof of pretext (Dean, 1983, p. 372).

(a) Prima Face Case of Disparate Treatment:
The plaintiff must initially show that he or she is a part of a protected group and was not treated the same as a member of a non-protected group (Steel, Guss, 2005). For example, if a disabled person is fired because of her disability, the employee can prove that her disability was a motivating factor for the employer's decision.

(b) Shifting Burden of Proof for a legitimate nondiscriminatory reason:

After establishing disparate treatment, the burden shifts to the defendant "to show a legitimate, non-discriminatory reason for the adverse action" (Steel, Guss, 2005). Defendant's burden is not huge, but the defendant must introduce evidence that is "legitimate," "nondiscriminatory," and "clear and reasonably specific" (Player, 1992, p. 75).

(c) Proof of pretext:

After presenting evidence of legitimate and nondiscriminatory reasons, the burden shifts to plaintiff to prove that the defendant's reason is a pretext for discrimination. In this case, the employee must present stronger evidence than presented in the prima facie case, in the initial establishment of the burden of proof (Steel, Guss, 2005).

Intentional Discrimination

To prove intentional discrimination, the employee must show that the employer was inclined to discriminate against members of a certain group (Steel, Guss, 2005). In *Wards Cove Packing v. Antonio* (1989) the Court held that the employee must show proof of intentional discrimination in claims of unlawful practices.[4]

Intentional discrimination is committed when "anyone who discriminates acts on the ground for the discrimination" (Rutherglen, 1995, p.128). For instance, when committing race discrimination, one cannot do so without taking race into account. Rutherglen (1995) emphasized that claims of intentional discrimination were successful in stressing discrimination patterns and segregation in employment, especially after the endorsement of Title VII. The Civil Rights Act of 1991 took further steps in improving remedies to victims of intentional discrimination, by including discrimination on grounds of race and other grounds such as protecting those who do not have jobs, minorities, and women. The Civil Rights Act of 1991 further amended sections of Title VII of the Civil Rights Act of 1964.

In *Fitzpatrick v. Bitzer*, the Supreme Court implied that Title VII's ban of intentional discrimination is valid under the Fourteenth Amendment which "forbids unjustified discrimination by state or local governments on the basis of race, religions, sex or national origin" (Dean, 372). However, in *Washington v. Davis* (1975) the Supreme Court ruled, "the interpretation of the Constitution was 'plain error' because the proof of discriminatory intent is a necessary element in proving a violation of fifth or

---

[4]   Refer to Table 8 for a complete discussion of *Wards Cove Packing. v. Antonio* (1989).

fourteenth amendment" (Dean, 393). In this case, black police officers filed a suit against officials of the District of Columbia who rejected their application.

The claim was that the Police Department discriminated on the basis of race, violating the Fifth Amendment. The officers argued that they were discriminated against because the department required them to take a verbal ability and reading test for the hiring process. The test disqualified a great number of blacks. However, in a 7–2 decision, the court of appeals held that the passing of the test was not sufficient in proving that the test was job related. Therefore, the Supreme Court decided that the officers failed to prove discriminatory intent.

Disparate Impact

Disparate Impact is considered a claim alleging unintentional discrimination and may be demonstrated with statistical proof. For example, in *Griggs v. Duke Power Co.,* the employer instituted a policy that appeared to be neutral regarding a protected group, but in practice applied them to discriminate against the group. Data census determined the impact of the high school diploma requirement. 34 % of the white workers had high school diplomas and only 12 % of African Americans completed high school.

Title VII of the Civil Rights Act of 1964 makes it unlawful for an employer to discriminate against individuals regarding hiring because of race, color, religion, sex or national origin. The Act also banned limiting, segregation or classification of employees that would adversely affect the employee. In *Griggs v. Duke Power Co.,* (1971), the employer required a high school diploma and a passing score on two tests.

The Supreme Court reverted the lower court's conclusion in requiring proof of discriminatory motive and stated that, Title VII "prohibits not only overt discrimination, but also practices that are fair in form, but discriminatory in practice" (*Griggs,* 1971). This liability is also known as "disparate-impact" theory and in practice may be seen as an infringement of Title VII without showing evidence of the employer's intent to discriminate.

(a)   Prima facie case of disparate impact:
The initial burden in a disparate impact case is on the plaintiff to demonstrate that the person has been harmed by employment practices.

(b)   Burden of Proof—Business Necessity:
Then the burden shifts to the defendant to justify the challenged claims. The Burden of proof demonstrates that the victim of the unlawful practices is subject to an adverse employment action. Although Title VII states that discrimination based on race is prohibited, the Supreme Court interpreted Title VII in *Griggs v. Duke Power Co.,* (1971), on basis of "business necessity." The business necessity questioned if the tests would negatively affect the

overall performance of the agency. However, *Wards Cove Packing v. Antonio* (1989) weakened the concept of business necessity (Player, 1992). After the plaintiff establishes that the practice has an adverse effect on the protected group, then:

> "The dispositive issue is whether the challenged practice serves, in a significant way, the legitimate goal of the employer... A mere insubstantial justification in this regard will not suffice... At the same time, though, there is no requirement that the challenged practice be 'essential' or 'indispensable' to the employer's business to pass muster." (*Wards Cover Packing Co., v. Antonio*, S. Ct. 1989)

More importantly, the Court held that the plaintiff's presentation of alternatives do not prove discriminatory practices. Instead they suggest rather than prove, illegal motivation for the use of the practices (Player, 1992, p. 9).

(c) Burden of Persuasion:

Finally, the burden shifts back to the plaintiff to demonstrate that the employer's employment decision is pretextual or not. In another case, in *Smith v. City of Jackson*, (2005) Smith claimed that the plan had an adverse impact on the older workers.[5] However, the department made the plan based on seniority, on the years of service, and not on the years of the employees. Therefore, the City's practices were unintentional to discriminate based on age. The Court's findings in *Wards Cove Packing Co. v. Antonio,* (1989) narrowed the scope of liability on "disparate impact." The required test in *Wards Cove* had an adverse impact on the workers.

The Civil Rights Act of 1991 overturned *Wards Cove Packing Co., v. Antonio* placing the burden upon the employer by interpreting "demonstrate" as to mean "meets the burdens of production and persuasion" and then making it unlawful practice where plaintiff shows that a specific policy caused disparate impact on the protected class, and failed to show business necessity (Player, 1993, p. 96). The burden falls on the defendant to establish the validity of the test, but adjusting test scores on the basis of race, sex, religion, or national origin violates CRA of 1991.

---

[5] See Table 9 for a complete overview of *Smith v. City of Jackson*, (2005).

Chapter 3
RESEARCH DESIGN

3.1 Method

Although many scholars have demonstrated a great deal of interest in the study of employment discrimination (Eastwood, 1972; Long, 1976; Roberts, 1985; Bardford, 1990; Deitch, 1993; Reskin, 2000; White, 2000), only a few have conducted empirical investigation to test the extent of the impact of government actions on employment discrimination (Hellriegel & Short, 1972; Hopkins, 1980; Donohue & Sigelman, 1991; Blumrosen 1999).

A major reason for the lack of empirical research in this area is that this influence is not easily measured. Donohue and Siegelman (1991) analyzed the socioeconomic and legal changes that may have provoked the rise of employment discrimination litigation (p. 984). Smith (1980) studied the relationship between employment actions and discrimination characteristics. According to Smith, "confusion, uncertainty and constant change in regulation and unstable body of law" has increased the need to reassess "the role of conciliation in enforcing compliance and procedural intricacies of the law" (Smith, 1980, p. 505). Other scholars compared the number of workers in various occupational categories to the number of minorities in those categories (Knapp and Kustis, 1996; Blumrosen, 1999).

The central research question seeks to answer: to what extent do laws, executive orders, and court decisions influence employment discrimination; and what is the nature of that influence? To study the relationship between the legislative law and the employment discrimination, multivariate analysis is used, to capitalize on benefits of both qualitative and quantitative method. Qualitative methodology allows the reader to better understand the nature of the influence of the legislative laws on employment discrimination.

To assess the extent to which government actions impact discrimination practices a timeline was formulated. This timeline is essential because it helps us examine the relationship between government action and employment discrimination. It also helps us find answers to key questions such as: Was Title VII of the Civil Rights Act of 1964 successful in prohibiting employment discrimination? Did Supreme Court decisions influence the rise or decrease of employment discrimination cases? What was the role of Executive Orders in employment discrimination?

Second, quantitative data is gathered to test the progress of employment discrimination. Table 12 shows changes in U. S. population from 1992–2004. In addition, it reveals changes of income status of the population, based on gender and race from 1992–2004. Table 13 shows EEOC trends of employment discrimination by type, on the basis of age, race, sex, sexual harassment, equal pay, religion and national origin. The numerical data consists of the total number of charges of employment discrimination by type, including charges filed and resolved under Title VII, ADA, ADEA, EPA.

The employment discrimination data used in this thesis came largely from two sources. First, data on U.S. resident population came from U.S. Census Bureau, Population Division from 1992 to 2004. Table 12 includes total U.S. population by gender and race and shows the number of households with earnings and total money income. Second, data on EEOC charges came from EEOC'S annual reports for the Fiscal Years 1992 through 2004. Table 13 includes the total number of charges and resolutions of employment discrimination based on age, disability, national origin, gender, pregnancy, equal pay, sexual harassment, race, and religion.

3.2 Development of the Model

3.2.1 Time Horizons

The timeline, as illustrated in Table 10, covers a time period from 1866–2005. The timeline lists relevant laws, executive orders, and court decisions for the designated time periods. Table 11 further breaks down landmark legislative and judicial decisions. Cases were selected considering their significance in employment discrimination on the basis of race, gender, religion, sex, national origin, disability, and age, and their impact in determining prima face cases, reasonable accommodation, hostile environment, and Title VII cases.

Although the numerical data as shown in Table 12 & 13, indicates a reduction from 1992–2004, the timeline covers a more extensive time period, beginning in 1866 and ending in 2005. The assumption of this study is that government actions, including legislative laws and Supreme Court decisions prior to 1992, had a direct impact on changes of employment discrimination subsequent to 1992.

The process of accumulating information, reviewing landmark Supreme Court cases, compiling numerical data, and producing the final document was far more involved than anticipated. However, the necessity of this kind of information is significant in answering the central research question, in understanding the relationship between government actions and the influence of employment discrimination.

Any attempt to understand the impact of government and Supreme Court involvement in employment discrimination must consider laws and policies formulated by the government and landmark Supreme Court cases. For example, variation around the general upward trend of employment discrimination may be due to the inconsistencies of Supreme Court decisions or the ineffectiveness of the law.

In particular, persons with disabilities received federal protection with the implementation of the Rehabilitation Act of 1973 and the Americans with Disability Act of 1990. Both statues prohibit employment discrimination against qualified individuals with disabilities. The Supreme Court's interpretations suggest that it was up to the Court to determine the scope of legislation, what qualifies as disability, what is a major life activity, what is reasonable accommodation, and what is considered discrimination under the statues (Barker L, Barker T, et al., 1999).

Until 1970s, there was little attention to the needs of disabled individuals in the workforce. The Rehabilitation Act of 1973 focused on improving the lives of those disabled in the workforce, however the Act was not successful "in integrating those with disability more fully into society" (Collignon, 1997, p. 130). Americans with Disabilities Act of 1990 (ADA) and Disability Discrimination Act of 1992

(DDA) corrected and improved the 1973 act. ADA and DDA prohibit employment discrimination on the basis of disability and focus on providing economic self-sufficiency, higher level of income, better health care and a higher standard of life for the disabled (Collignon, 1997). The Rehabilitation Act of 1973 was later amended in 1998, including federal sector employees.

Given the likelihood of controversy in the issue, which would question the effectiveness of the law, there is substantial evidence, (illustrated in Figure 2 and in Table 2,) which suggests that government interference makes a difference in employment discrimination. Legislative decisions such as ADA expanded the number of workers who were protected by civil rights legislation, especially between 1994 and 2004. The effects of legislative and judicial decisions are estimated in Chapter 4.

3.2.2 Measures

The second part of this analysis includes an evaluation of quantitative data. The numerical data shown in Table 13 provides essential data to employment discrimination and offers information on significant trends and issues arising from employment discrimination. EEOC defines employment discrimination as unlawful treatment and practices in the workforce on the basis of six variables: (1) age, (2) disability, (3) national origin, (4) sex, (5) race, and (6) religion. In addition, population change and income status of U.S. population are considered because they serve as a link to understanding the trends in employment discrimination.

Age Discrimination: EEOC refers to section 11 of the Age Discrimination in Employment Act of 1967 in interpreting laws in age discrimination cases. The ADEA protects persons against age discrimination in employment practices such as hiring, firing, promotion, layoff, compensation, benefits, job assignments and training. Any individual who is 40 years of age or older is protected by the ADEA against unlawful employment practices. The ADEA applies to employers with 20 or more employees, employment agencies labor organizations and other agencies.

More important, the U.S. Federal Code, Title 29, Sec. 621 (1994) titled "Age Discrimination in Employment" clearly states that it is unlawful to discriminate against a person because of his/her age. 29 U.S.C. 621 specifically gave protection to the employees discriminated on the basis of age and banned age discrimination. Thus, the level of age discrimination filed charges should exhibit lower numbers. Therefore, the following hypothesis is forwarded:

> *Hypothesis 1.* U.S. Federal Code, Title 29, Sec. 621 will significantly impact the total received number of charges of age discrimination and legislative

law, and the result will be such that the number of charges will be lower after 1994 when the statue was implemented.

Disability Discrimination: Under the Americans with Disability Act of 1990 (ADA) disabled persons were protected against disability discrimination. Doyle (1997) defined disability as a physical or mental impairment. White (2000) argued that ADA is "a broadly worded statue," therefore its implementation would require various agencies "to flesh out its terms" (p. 535). However, as of July 1994, employers with 15 or more employees are covered under ADA. Thus, the coverage of employees expanded.

The Disability Discrimination Act of 1995 (DDA), strengthened the ADA, and narrowed the definition of a qualified disabled person. DDA emphasized on the "long term adverse effect on [the disabled person's] ability to carry out normal day-to-day activities (Doyle, 1997, p. 65). ADA extended coverage to employers with fifteen employees, thus it suggests that the law allowed for more employees to file discrimination charges. Therefore, the following hypothesis is forwarded:

> ***Hypothesis 2.*** ADA moderates the relationship between legislative law and the total number of disability discrimination charges

such that the number of filed charges will be higher after 1994, with the implementation of the 1994 law.

National Origin Discrimination: Section 703(a)(1) of Title VII and 42 U.S.C. § 2000e-2(a) prohibit employment discrimination because of birthplace, ancestry, culture, or linguistic characteristics of a nationality. Title VII states that no one can be denied of equal employment opportunity because of his or her national origin. The Act applies to employers with fifteen or more employees and bans discrimination on the basis of nationality or citizenship.

In *EEOC v. Synchro-Start Prods. Inc*, 29 F. Supp. 2d 911, 914–15 (N.D. Ill. 1999) the court ruled that the English-only rules can create discriminatory work environment based on national origin. This decision allowed for more employees to file for national origin discrimination. Thus, the following hypothesis is forwarded:

> ***Hypothesis 3:*** *EEOC v. Synchro-Start Prods. Inc,* (N.D. Ill. 1999) will have a significant impact on the number of national origin discrimination charges, such that the number of charges will increase after 1999, when the court decided.

Sex Discrimination: Title VII of the Civil Rights Act of 1964 prohibits employment discrimination on the basis of sex, referring to gender, not to sexuality or sexual orientation, including pregnancy, childbirth or related conditions (as amended by the Pregnancy Discrimination Act (PDA); equal pay for equal work of man and women (as stated in the Equal Pay Act of 1963), and sexual harassment (prohibiting sexual favors in the workplace). Title VII includes compensation protection on the basis of sex discrimination, in practices of hiring, firing, promoting, training, and other practices.

In *Harris v. Forklift Systems* (1993), the Supreme Court held to have applied incorrect standards under Title VII of the Civil Rights Act of 1964 in denying a female worker's claim that discrimination because of her gender caused an abusive work environment. The Court determines the hostile or abusive environment by looking at evidence that shows physical threatening or humiliating or unreasonable interference with the employee's work performance.

In addition, the effect on the employee's psychological well-being is relevant in determining a hostile or abusive work environment, but it is not required. This meant that sex discrimination could be proved without showing psychological harm. This removed the burden of showing emotional harm. Thus, the decision expanded coverage for victims of sex discrimination. Therefore, the following hypothesis is forwarded:

Hypothesis 4: The Supreme Court's decision in *Harris v. Forklift Systems* (1993), will be directly related to the charges of sex discrimination, and the result will be such that the number of sex charges will be higher after 1993 when the Court decided on the case.

Racial Discrimination: Title VII of the Civil Rights Act of 1964 protects individuals from discrimination on the basis of race and color. Title VII states that it is unlawful (1) to discriminate because of race-related characteristics and conditions, (2) to harass on the basis of color and race, (3) to segregate and classify employees on such basis, and (4) require pre-employment inquiries that will suggest that the employer will make employment decisions on the basis of race. Thus, an employee cannot reject an employee's application due to race and color.

However, keeping in mind the historical discourse on race in the South, equal opportunity for whites and blacks and individuals of other ethnic backgrounds has implied unlawful practices on the basis of race. Deitch (1993) argued that race has been central to the civil rights movement in the 40's and 50's. Interpretation of race and color in the past is "in a way that has discriminated against" such characteristics, especially women (p. 196). Deitch

(1993) concluded that race and class interrupt the shaping of state action or political influence (p. 200).

In 1995, the Rehnquist Court placed restrictions on the use of race-based remedies in federal contracting activities in *Adarand Constructor, Inc. v. Pena* (1995). This narrowed the scope of employment discrimination. This suggests that the coverage of the law was limited, and fewer employees were eligible to file discrimination charges. Therefore, the following hypothesis is forwarded:

> ***Hypothesis 5***: *Adarand Constructor, Inc. v. Pena* (1995) influenced the number of race discrimination charges, by reducing the number of charges after 1995, with the decision of the Supreme Court in *Adarand*.

> ***Religious Discrimination***: The First Amendment provides protection against religious expression. In addition, Title VII of the Civil Rights of 1964 prohibits discrimination of employees on the basis of religious beliefs or practices.

> "The term "religion" includes all aspects of religious observance and practice, as well as belief, unless an employer demonstrates that he is unable to reasonably accommodate to an employee's or

prospective employee's religious observance or practice without undue hardship on the conduct of the employer's business." [Title VII, Section 701(j)]

More importantly, the Religious Freedom Restoration Act of 1993 (RFRA), signed by President Clinton focused on preventing laws that significantly burden individuals to free religious expression. Thus, it would sound logical that that this government action would reduce the number of religious charges. However, it also meant that RFRA would modify the state laws, which would violate Congress's power. Thus, RFRA caused tension with the Courts (Kimball & Anderson, 1999). Consequently, many states implemented their own RFRA laws. This questions the validity of the Courts and government in their efforts to stop discrimination. Thus, the following hypothesis is forwarded:

> ***Hypothesis 6:*** The Religious Freedom Restoration Act of 1993 will directly impact the total number of religious discrimination charges, by increasing the number of charges after 1993, with the implementation of RFRA.

Chapter 4
FINDINGS AND DISCUSSION

Age Discrimination

The Age Discrimination in Employment Act of 1967 (ADEA) prohibits employment discrimination on the basis of age. Individuals who are 40 years or older are protected under ADEA. In addition, U.S. Federal Code, Title 29, Sec. 621, provides further protection. Effective in January, 1, 1994, the federal code prohibited employers from arbitrary discrimination because of age, promotes employment of older persons based on their ability rather than age, and helps employers find solutions to problems taking place from the influence of age on employment.

Previous government actions, U.S.C.§ 29 (621) in particular, have lowered the number of charges of age discrimination. Table 13 reveals the total number of received and resolved charges of age discrimination. In Fiscal Year 1993, EEOC received 19,809 receipts filed under ADEA, Title VII, ADA and/or EPA and resolved 19,809 age discrimination charges. The number of received charges was dramatically reduced to 14,141 in FY 1999. Figure 1 provides data that shows EEOC age discrimination charges, including received and solved from FY 1992–2004.

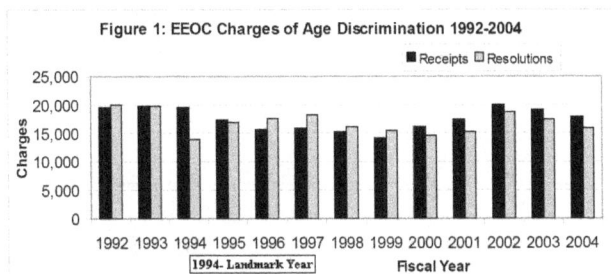

Figure 1: EEOC Charges of Age Discrimination 1992-2004

EEOC's data is useful in understanding trends of charges of age discrimination, but it doesn't explain what exactly accounts for the decline. However, the regression analysis in Table 1 establishes and tests the relationship between government actions and number of charges of age discrimination. These findings **support hypothesis # 1**.

Table 1 presents findings relevant to the employment discrimination argument, where age discrimination is the dependent variable. There is strong evidence that suggests that U.S.C.§ 29 (621) is the indicator of the decrease of charges of age discrimination. The average number of charges for any given year after 1994 decreased by 2,585. The average of all receipts is 17,504 and the standard deviation is 1994, suggesting that the lasting impact of this legislation is substantial.

In this case, government action did have a strong influence in employment discrimination on the basis of age, by reducing the number of discrimination charges after U.S.C.§ 29 (621) was implemented.

Table 1 **Regression Analysis over EEOC charges of age discrimination from 1992–2004**

	Age Discrimination Charges
Constant	19691.00**
	(1286.07)
Independent Variable:	
U.S. Federal Code, 29(621)	-2585.09*
	(1398.1)
R^2	0.237
N	13

Dependent Variable: Age Discrimination
B signifies the Unstandardized Coefficients
* significant at .10
** significant at .05

Disability Discrimination

Table 13 shows the total number of charges filed of disability discrimination under Title VII, ADA and DDA. In 1992, EEOC received 1,048 charges and in 1995 the number of disability charges increased drastically to 19,798, out of which, 18,900 were solved. However, as Figure 2 shows, after 1995 the number of disability charges was significantly reduced. In 2004, the number dropped to 15,376 receipts.

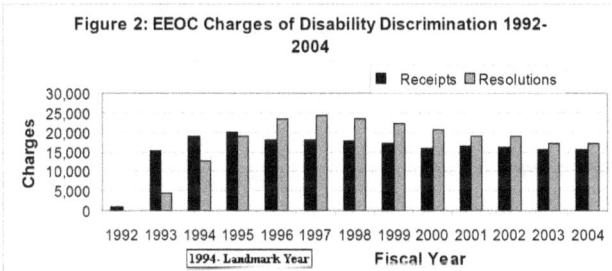

Figure 2: EEOC Charges of Disability Discrimination 1992-2004

EEOC's data is valuable in determining trends in employment discrimination on the basis of disability, however, it is impossible to point out which law in particular is responsible for the decrease or increase of the disability charges. The regression analysis shows good evidence in favor of the hypothesis of disability discrimination. The average number of charges in any given year after 1994 increased by 8,991. Considering that the average of all receipts is 15,769 with a standard of deviation of 4654, the impact of the ADA is quite substantial. These findings support hypothesis # 2.

Table 2 shows that there is reasonable evidence that suggests that ADA as implemented in 1994 accounts for the drastic increase of disability charges. This means that the law widened the scope of protection to agencies with fifteen or more employees, allowing more victims of disability discrimination to file charges.

Table 2 Regression Analysis over EEOC charges of disability discrimination from 1992–2004

	Disability Discrimination Charges
Constant	8161.00**
	(2365.54)
Independent Variables:	
ADA as implemented in 1994	8991.27**
	(2571.61)
R^2	0.526
N	13

Dependent Variable: Disability Discrimination
B signifies the Unstandardized Coefficients
* significant at .10
** significant at .05

National Origin Discrimination

EEOC defines national origin discrimination based on (1) the individual's ancestor's place of origin, (2) the individual's physical, cultural or linguistic characteristics of a national origin group, (3) individual's accent and (4) individual's association with persons of a national origin group. Figure 3 illustrates the changes in the national origin discrimination charges filed under Title VII. In 1993, EEOC received 7,454 charges of national origin discrimination and the number of charges dropped down to 6,687 in 1996. After 1999, the number of charges increased up to 9,046 in 2002.

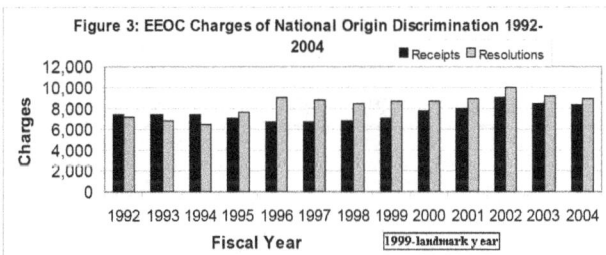

Figure 3: EEOC Charges of National Origin Discrimination 1992-2004

Figure 3 shows mixed results, by illustrating both increases and decreases in the number of national origin discrimination charges. The regression analysis in Table 3 suggests EEOC v. Synchro-Start Prods. (1999) contributed to the increase of national origin charges. The average number of national origin discrimination charges for any given year after 1999 increased by 1,257.

The average of all receipts of national origin discrimination charges is 7,561, with a standard deviation of 738. This suggests a moderate increase in charges filed as a result of this Court decision and lends **support to hypothesis # 3**.

The regression analysis shows good evidence in support of the hypothesis of the national origin discrimination. In this case the court determined that EEOC's claims of requiring English during work hours, had a disparate impact on employees who come from Non-English-speaking countries. This allowed for more employees to file national origin discrimination charges.

Table 3 Regression Analysis over EEOC charges of national origin discrimination from 1992–2004

National Origin Discrimination Charges

Constant	7077.75**
	(137.80)
Independent Variables:	
EEOC v. Synchro-Start Prods. (1999) 1257.05**	
(222.19)	
R²	0.744
N	13

Dependent Variable: National Origin Discrimination
B signifies the Unstandardized Coefficients
* significant at .10; ** significant at .05

The results in Table 3 suggest that *EEOC v. Synchro-Start Prods.* (N.D. Ill. 1999) has a direct relationship with the increase of charges.[6]

Sex Discrimination

The total number of sex discrimination charges on the basis of gender, equal pay, sexual harassment, and pregnancy-related discrimination filed under Title VII are shown in Figure 4 & 5. These figures show mixed trends as the frequency of discrimination tended to vary according to the type of sex discrimination. For instance, in 1993 EEOC received 23,919 sex discrimination charges on the basis of gender.

The number of charges increased to 25,860 in FY 1994, and up to 26,181 in 1995. EEOC received 1,328 sex discrimination charges on the basis of equal pay. The number dropped down to 969 in 1996 and increased up to 1,256 in 2002. Sex discrimination charges on the basis of pregnancy showed mixed results as well; the number of charges increased up to 4,191 in 1995 and dropped down to 3,732 the following year and increasing again in 2002 with 4,714 charges.

---

[6]   However, EEOC v. Synchro-Start Prods. (N.D. Ill. 1999) does not account for the other changes in the number of charges filed under Title VII. Immigrant population and labor force changes and workplace language are considered to explain the varied results of national origin discrimination charges.

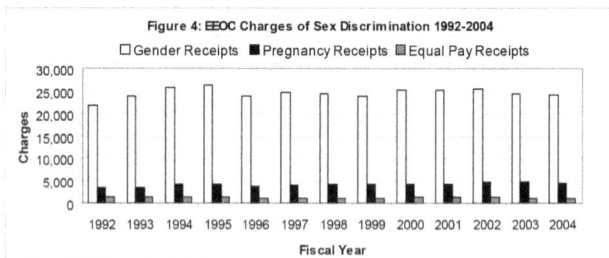

Figure 4: EEOC Charges of Sex Discrimination 1992-2004

However, in 1992, EEOC received 10,532 sexual harassment discrimination charges, and in 1993 the charges totaled to 11,908. As Figure 5 illustrates, the number of sexual harassment discrimination increased up to 15,889 in fiscal year 1997. In 2004 EEOC received 13,136 charges of sexual harassment and resolved 13,786 sexual harassment charges. 15.1% of the received charges were filed by males.

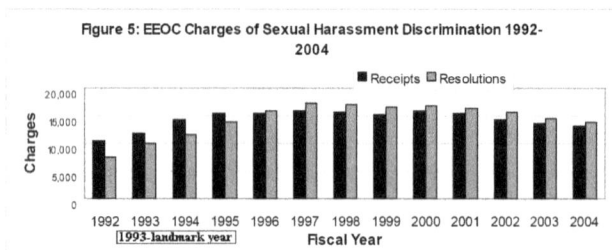

Figure 5: EEOC Charges of Sexual Harassment Discrimination 1992-2004

The general definition of sex discrimination includes unlawful treatment on the basis of gender, pregnancy, equal pay, and sexual harassment. *Harris v. Forklift Systems* (1993) influenced the increase of charges of sex discrimination on the basis of gender and sexual harassment.

The same effect cannot be said for the other definitions of sex discrimination since results varied. *Harris v. Forklift Systems* (1993) doesn't show enough evidence to interpret the variations in wage and pregnancy-based discrimination. Considering changes in population and income between men and women might help explain the variations in sex discrimination. Figure 6 shows the number of male and female population in U.S., and the number of male and female households with earnings.

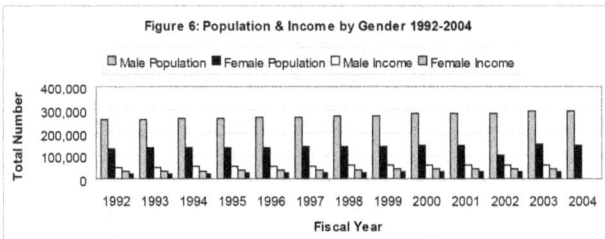

Figure 6: Population & Income by Gender 1992-2004

Figure 6 shows that the female population is higher than the male population. In 1993, there are 125,800 men, and 131,983 women. However, the number of women households with income earning is less than the men's. In 1993, there are only 33,524 women households with income earnings, and 49,818 men household with income earning. This shows that the women population is higher than the men's however, the number of women with income earning is les then the men. Therefore, this could account for sex employment discrimination on the basis of equal pay, because of equal pay disparities that exist between men and women.

More importantly, EEOC's data emphasizes fiscal year 1993 as a significant date for sex discrimination, with the number of gender and sexual harassment discrimination charges increased in years following 1993. However, this analysis is limited in providing for specific phenomena that accounts for such changes.

The regression analysis revealed that in fact, the Supreme Court case *Harris v. Forklift Systems* (1993) is vital in sex discrimination, particularly in gender and sexual harassment discrimination charges. Table 4 shows data that suggest that *Harris v. Forklift Systems* has a direct relationship with the increase of the charges of gender and sexual harassment discrimination.

The average number of charges in any given year after 1993 on the basis of sexual harassment increased by 4,164. The average of all receipts is 14,376 with a standard deviation of 1665. The average number of charges on the basis of gender in any given year after 1993 increased by 2,983. The average of all receipts of gender discrimination is 2,549, with a standard deviation of 1126. The regression analysis gives strong evidence **in favor of the hypothesis # 4**.

Table 4 Regression Analysis over EEOC charges of sexual discrimination from 1992–2004

Sex Discrimination Charges[7]

	Sexual Harassment	Gender
Constant	10532**	21796 **
	(1252.31)	(798.06)
Independent Variables:		
*Harris v. Forklift Systems (*1993)	4164.42**	2982.58**
	(1303.44)	(830.65)
R^2	0.481	0.540
N	13	13

Dependent Variable: Sex Discrimination

B signifies the Unstandardized Coefficients

* significant at .10; ** significant at .05

---

[7] This regression analysis is limited because the data set starts with FY 1992. The purpose of Table 4 is to report the data and not to strongly conclude. However, Figure 5 shows clear trends of sex discrimination in support of hypothesis # 4.

Racial Discrimination

The EEOC received 29,986 charges and in 1995 and the number of disability charges decreased to 26,287 the following year. Figure 6 shows, after 1995 the number of disability charges was gradually reduced. In 1996, the number of racial discrimination charges was 29,199, and continued to reduce afterwards.

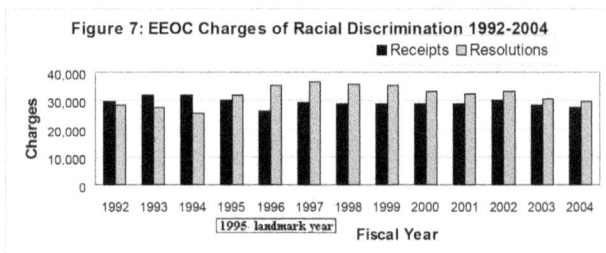

Figure 7: EEOC Charges of Racial Discrimination 1992-2004

The hypothesis of race discrimination charges stated that *Adarand Constructor, Inc. v. Pena (1995)* had a direct relationship with the number of charges, and the charges of race discrimination will reduce after 1995. The regression analysis provides data that supports the hypothesis. Table 5 shows good evidence that suggests that *Adarand Constructor, Inc. v. Pena* (1995) accounts for the decrease of race discrimination charges.

Table 5 Regression Analysis over EEOC charges of race discrimination from 1992–2004

	Race Discrimination Charges
Constant	2966.33**
	(366.72)
Independent Variables:	
Adarand Constructor, Inc. v. Pena (1995)	-2256.33*
	(725.97)
R^2	0.468
N	13

Dependent Variable: Race Discrimination
B signifies the Unstandardized Coefficients
* significant at .10
** significant at .05

The average number of charges on the race discrimination, for any given year after 1995 decreased by 2,256. The average of all receipts is 29,230 and the standard deviation is 1447. The negative coefficient suggests that fewer employees were eligible to file for racial employment discrimination, because the Supreme Court's decision in *Adarand Constructor, Inc. v. Pena* (1995) narrowed the scope of employment discrimination. The regression analysis gives strong evidence **in favor hypothesis #5**.

It is important to note the increase of the number of race discrimination charges in FY 1997.

With the exception of FY 1997, charges of race discrimination are lower after 1995. In 1996, the number of charges was reduced to 26,287, however, in 1997 the number of race discrimination charges increased up to 29,199. Perhaps the population and income changes play a role. In 1997, there are 22,1333 whites, 33,989 African Americans, 29,182 Hispanics and 10,135 Asians, in the United States. This shows the great disparities that exist between the number of households with income earning among different racial groups.

In 1997, there are approximately 77,936 white households with income earnings; 12,474 African Americans; 8,590 Hispanics and only 3,125 Asians with income earnings. This shows huge gaps between population of the different racial groups and the economic status. Perhaps, the economic disparity is the reason for the increase of race discrimination charges in 1997. After 1997, the number of race discrimination charges reduces down to 27,696 in 2004.

Religious Discrimination

In 1992 EEOC received 1,388 religious discrimina-tion charges filed under Title VII of the Civil Rights Act of 1964. After 1993, the number of charges on the basis of religious harassment increased contin-uously. In 1996 EECO received 1,564 charges and resolved 1911 files. In 2003, the EEOC number of religious discrimination charges increased up to 2,532, out of which 2,690 were resolved.

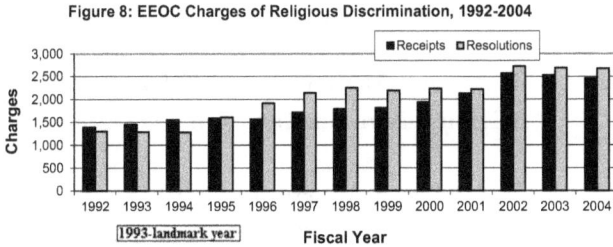

Figure 8: EEOC Charges of Religious Discrimination, 1992-2004

EEOC data as illustrated in Figure 8, shows that after 1993 there is a constant change in the number of religious harassment charges. In fact, the increase of the filed charges continues up to Fiscal Year 2003. Results in Table 6 show good evidence, supporting hypothesis # 6. Indeed, the RFRA has an impact on the increase of the number of charges. The average number of charges, for any given year after 1993 was increased by 548. Since the average number of total receipts is 1,882, with a standard deviation of 416, the impact of the RFRA is quite substantial.

The research's findings indicate that indeed the impact of government actions and Supreme Court decisions on trends of employment discrimination practices is quite substantial. For instance, the average number of disability charges in any given year after 1994 increased by 8,991. The positive coefficient means that the law expanded the definition of the terms, therefore, allowing more people to be eligible to file discriminatory practices. Considering that the number of disability charges increased notably, the impact of the law is very significant. The coverage was expanded to employers with 15 or more employees, the law covered more employees.

Table 6 Regression Analysis over EEOC charges of religious discrimination from 1992–2004.

	Religious Discrimination [8] Charges
Constant	1418.50*
	(267.55)
Independent Variable:	
The Religious Freedom Restoration Act of 1993	548.09**
	(290.86)
R^2	0.244
N	13

Dependent Variable: Religious Discrimination
B signifies the Unstandardized Coefficients
* significant at .10
** significant at .05

Government action curbed age discrimination. The average number of age discrimination charges

---

[8]   This regression analysis is limited because of the data set. However, EEOC data clearly indicates that the volume of religious discrimination charges has increased since 1992 with 1,388 charges to a peak of 2,466 in 2004.

for any given year after 1994 decreased by 2,585. The negative coefficient indicates that that law inhibited individuals from filing discriminatory charges. In this case, 29 U.S.C. 621 narrowed the pool of eligible individuals who would be covered under the law. Considering that fewer people could file for employment discrimination, the number of discrimination charges decreased. The same effect was seen in the racial discrimination charges. The average number of charged for any given year after 1995 decreased 2,256.

However, in the cases of national origin and sex discrimination practices, even though regression analysis strongly suggested that the law was accountable for the increase of discrimination charges, the same could not be argued for the varying types of the discriminatory practices. For example, *Forklift* showed that after 1993 gender and sexual harassment charges reduced, but the argument is not true for equal pay or pregnancy charges of the sex discrimination type.

The research suggests that other factors such as increase of population, labor force and income status, could be accountable for the mixed results in the cases of national origin and sex discrimination cases. U.S. Census Bureau reported that between 1990 and 2000, the proportion of the U.S. population of minorities, specifically Hispanic and Asian origin increased significantly (U.S. Census Bureau, 1990). Stephan and Bachman (2000) argued that diversity in the workforce has increased as a result of the increase of population of particular national origin groups.

The Immigrant Labor Force reported that in 1999, immigrant workers numbered 15.7 million, accounting for 12 percent of U.S. workers. Between 1990 and 1998, 12.7 million new jobs were opened in the United States, and 38 percent (5.1 million) of the employees were immigrants (Immigrant Labor Force, 2000). Equal Employment Opportunity Commission reported that in 2000, Hispanics, Asians, and American Indians constituted 15.2 percent of the workforce in the private sector (EEOC, 2000). The increase of immigrant labor force may constitute for the lack of proper guidance of addressing diversity. As a result, more employers violated Title VII.

Chapter 5
CONCLUSION

Legislative and judicial decisions have made a difference in employment discrimination charges filed. This research shows that government intervention on employment discrimination has a direct influence in trends and changes of equal employment opportunity practices. The volume of employment discrimination charges has grown substantially over the last 13 years—from 1,048 disability charges in FY 1992 to a peak of about 15,376 charges in 2004; from 10,532 sexual harassment charges in 1992 to a maximum of 15,889 in 1996. The overall employment discrimination charges have grown rapidly, with periods of substantial growth and exceptional decline. For instance, in FY 1992, EEOC received 29,548 racial discrimination charges to peak of 31,656 in 1994, to a dip of 27,696 in 2004.

Today, discrimination still exists in the workplace, despite the continuing efforts of the government and the Supreme Court to stop unlawful practices. In the wake of the #Me Too Movement more employers are beginning to provide additional training about improper and inappropriate behavior at the workplace. In 2018 EEOC released the staggering new numbers of on-the-job harassment complaints.

However, Congress and the Supreme Court have not always stood on common grounds when interpreting Title VII of the Civil Rights Act of 1964. It has been the responsibility of EEOC, the Supreme Court, the Congress, and other agencies given authority by the Congress to provide a workplace free of discrimination in the private and public sectors. Many vital laws such as Title VII, ADEA, ADA, DDA, Equal Pay Act, etc., were created and further amended to ensure equal opportunity for all individuals.

In 1967, the Age Discrimination Act (ADEA) promoted job opportunities for older workers based on their ability rather than age. Section VII of the ADEA specifies the prohibition against age discrimination. It is unlawful for an employer to refuse to hire an employee due to his or her age. In 1974, Congress extended coverage of ADEA to government agencies with twenty employees. This research shows that government actions have played a major role in curbing employment discrimination on the basis of age. U.S.C.§ 29 (621) played a pivotal role in reducing the age discrimination charges and provided protection for workers.

The Equal Pay Act of 1963 prohibited discrimination on the basis of sex in the payment of wages or benefits for equal work in the same working conditions and establishments. In addition, Title VII of the Civil Rights Act of 1964 and Title I of Americans with Disabilities Act of 1990 (ADA) and ADEA protect employees from equal pay and compensation discrimination. These laws prohibit compensation discrimination on the basis of race, color, disability, religion, sex, national origin, and age. EPA is the only law that requires the jobs to be substantially equal or in the same establishment.

Unlike EPA, Title VII, ADA, and ADEA do not make these specifications, therefore, they allow for compensation discrimination. For example, in cases such as an employer's compensation policy that has an adverse impact on the workers and is not job-related or implies business necessity. In other cases, pay differentials are allowed on the basis of merit, seniority, or a factor other than gender. In addition, the Pregnancy Discrimination Act, Title VII, the Family and Medical Leave Act, and ADA protect employees who are discriminated on the basis of pregnancy, childbirth or related medical conditions.

The Pregnancy Discrimination Act applies to employers with fifteen employees or more and protects women who are pregnant and states that the employees should be treated the same as other employees with same limitations or abilities. For example, it would be unlawful for an employer to refuse to hire a woman due to her pregnancy. If the employee requires maternity leave or is unable to perform her job due to the pregnancy, the employee must treat the woman the same as any other employee who is temporarily disabled. In addition, pregnancy benefits are not limited to married persons only under

Title VII. However, this issue has created controversy because it has raised the question of the fair treatment when men and women cannot be treated the same in this case.

Another implication that has caused a great controversy is the sexual harassment discrimination. "Quid Pro Quo" harassment is a form of sex discrimination on the basis of sexual harassment. In this case, the plaintiff must prove that the employer based his or her decision because of rejection or submission of unwelcome conduct (Steel, Guss, 2005). If employees have defined benefits and if the employer offers conditions or terms of employment for the employee to receive the benefits, then the employer is violating Title VII on the basis of sexual harassment. In this case, the court has to determine whether the employers may be held liable for such practices by employees.

"Hostile work environment" is another form of sex discrimination based on sexual harassment. In harassment cases it is not necessary to prove physical contact to determine a hostile environment. Sexual harassment jokes can account for one. "Unlike quid pro quo cases, employers are not strictly liable for all claims of harassment" (Steel and Guss, 2005). EEOC has determined that employers may be accountable and liable for harassment of their employees. Although, Title VII does not mention harassment, it has been argued that it prevents discrimination on the basis of membership to a particular group (Steel, and Guss, 2005).

For example, Title VII indicates that it prohibits employers from discrimination on the basis of national origin, as well as protects persons who are associated with a person of a particular national origin. National origin discriminating means treating an employee less favorably because he/she has a particular national origin. The Immigration Reform and Control Act of 1986 banned discrimination on the base of national origin and is enforced by the Office of Special Counsel for Immigration-Related Unfair Employment Practices at the Department of Justice (EEOC, 2002). Title VII covers employers with 15 employees. The Immigration Reform and Control Act of 1986 covers employers with four to fourteen employees. An employer is prohibited to make employment decisions on the basis of the worker's linguistic characteristics or has an accent of a particular national origin group.

The Immigration Reform and Control Act (IRCA) of 1986 requires employers to follow the procedures in ensuring the legality and permit of work in U.S. However, if an employer gives preferences to a U.S citizen in hiring or promotion opportunities, and clearly imposes citizenship requirement, then the employer is violating IRCA. An employer cannot reject an employee's application due to his citizenship. Thus, the employee is protected under Title VII.

In summary, government laws have created tensions because of broad and unclear language and because of the changing scope of discrimination. Such tensions should be solved by using a united effort and a common ideology in eradicating employment discrimination. The rules and the guidelines implemented by Congress should not be creating tensions; nor should they limit Supreme Court's role in curbing employment discrimination. In addition, government actions and Court's decision should provide fair treatment for all to maintain harmony in the workforce.

Despite the debate over the effectiveness of the Supreme Court and the government, legislative and judicial decisions have played an essential role in the growth of employment discrimination charges filed. First, the number of age discrimination charges decreased after the implementation of 29 U.S.C. 621, as the protected labor force grew. Second, the implementation of ADA in 1994 has had a major effect on the volume of disability discrimination charges filed, explaining an increase by 8991 in any given year after 1994.

Third, *EEOC v. Synchro-Start Prods. Inc.,* (1999) has clearly had an important influence on the volume of national origin discrimination charges. The court's ruling allowed for more workers to be protected after 1999. Fourth, differences in population and income by gender and race have had an important influence in the increase on the volume of racial and sex discrimination charges. Furthermore, immigrant labor force has had an influential role in racial and religious employment discrimination charges.

The government and the Supreme Court have put forth great efforts in banning employment discrimination practices, however, many challenges in interpreting the law have created a lot of controversy. Furthermore, political issues have been raised over judicial authority and the implementation of the law. This implies considerable effort is still needed to curb employment discrimination.

5.1 Landmark Judicial and Legislative Decisions

This section includes a summary of the following important cases: *Griggs v. Duke Power Co. (1971), Wards Cove Packing v. Antonio (1989),* and *Smith v. City of Jackson, Miss. (2005).* Table 11 shows an extensive summary in chronological order of the landmark judicial and legislative decisions on employment discrimination. Additionally, it includes a timeline of equal employment opportunity actions covering the period of 1866-2005. In Griggs v. Duke Power Co. (1971), Duke's internal transfer policy between departments was challenged by Griggs. The tests imposed by Duke Powers rendered many African American workers ineligible for transfers, promotions, or employment. The Supreme Court held that the intelligence tests must measure job performance ability. The unanimous decision by the Court set the legal precedent for "disparate-impact" lawsuits, involving racial discrimination claims.

Table 7: Case Overview: Griggs v. Duke Power Co. (1971)

GRIGGS V. DUKE POWER COMPANY
401 U.S. 424 (1971)

Argued: December 12, 1970

Decided: March 8, 1971

Subject: Civil Rights: Employment Discrimination

Facts of the Case:

Duke Power Company required a minimum of high school education and passing of the Mechanical Comprehension Test for their hiring and transferring standard, prior to the 1964 Act. Petitioner Willie Griggs challenged the company's policy and filed a suit on behalf of all African Americans employees. Duke claimed that the policy of the company discriminated against blacks and it violated Title VII of the Civil Rights Act of 1964.

Legal Question:

Did Duke Power Company violate Title VII in their hiring policy by requiring (a) high school education, and (b) minimum scores on two aptitude tests? Are these two factors requirements of discrimination?

Conclusions:

Decision: 8–0. The District Court dismissed the claims. The Court of Appeals concluded that Duke Company did not implement any discriminatory practices based on the argument of "to improve the overall qualification of the workforce." The court argued that as long as the tests were not designed to discriminate on the basis of race, then they could be used. Griggs failed to show such connection; therefore, the court allowed the company the use of the tests. The Supreme Court granted certiorari.

Table 8: Case Overview: Wards Cove Packing v. Antonio (1989)

WARDS COVE PACKING CO. V. ANTONIO 490 U.S. 642 (1989)

Argued:	January 18, 1989
Decided:	June 5, 1989

Facts of the Case:

Antonio, who was a nonwhite cannery worker filed against the Wards Co. claiming "disparate impact" under Title VII, based on four criteria: (1) nepotism in hiring, (2) failure to post noncannery openings, (3) rehiring preferences, and (4) an English requirement. The case went to the District Court, and later to the Supreme Court.

Legal Question:

Did Title VII of the Civil Rights Act of 1964 include "disparate impact" claims?

Conclusions:

Decision: 5–4. The claims were rejected by the District Court for failure of proof. "Objective Employment Practices" must carry proof for the courts to consider the claims seriously. The 9th Circuit agreed to hear the case en banc and found that the District Court had made an error. The Court concluded that the plaintiff showed disparate impact by describing the criteria of the employment unlawful practices. Therefore, the burden fell on the plaintiff to show the proof. However, the 9th Circuit sent it back to the District Court to evaluate if business necessity played a role, since the plaintiff did not put forth enough evidence to show discrimination. The Supreme Court concluded in a very weak decision. The dissented opinion judges stated that it was hard to prove business necessity and business justification.

Table 9: Case Overview: Smith v. City of Jackson, Miss. (2005)

SMITH V. CITY OF JACKSON, MISS. 03–1160 U.S. (2005)

Argued: November 3, 2004   Decided: March 30, 2005

Facts of the Case:

Azel Smith, who is an employee over the age of 40, as well as other employees of the same criteria, filed a suit in the federal district court against the police department of the City of Jackson in Mississippi. Smith claimed that the police department violated the Age Discrimination Employment Act of 1967 (ADEA). ADEA prohibits agencies from discriminating on the basis of age. The group claimed that, "they were adversely affected by the plan because of their age" (Smith, 2005). The plan gave officers with less then five years larger raises than those with more seniority, who were over 40.

Legal Question:

Does the Age Discrimination Employment Act of 1967 (ADEA) include "disparate impact claims?"

Conclusions:

The Fifth Circuit Court of Appeals ruled that disparate impact claims could not be made under ADEA. The Federal District Court affirmed the decision of the Court of Appeals arguing that "the claims are categorically unavailable under the ADEA, but it assumed that the facts alleged by petitioners would entitle them to relief under *Griggs v. Duke Power Co.*" (Smith, 2005). However, other federal courts of appeals ruled on the opposite. The officers with less seniority were granted "proportionately greater raises then those with seniority, and most officers over 40 had more than 5 years of service."

Table 10: Equal Employment Opportunity Actions Timeline 1866–2005

1866   Civil Rights Act of 1866

1870   Civil Rights Act of 1870

1871   Civil Rights Act of 1971

1875   Civil Rights Act of 1875

1896   *Plessy v. Ferguson* [163 U.S. 537 (1896)]

1954   *Brown v. Board of Education I* [347 U.S. 483 (1954)]

1955   Brown v. Board of Education II [347 U.S. 483 (1955)]

1961   Executive Order 10925 "Establishing the President's Committee on EEO"
        Poe v. Ullman [367 U.S. 497, 543 (1961)]

1963   The Fair Labor Standards Act in 1963

1964   Civil Rights Act of 1964

1965   Executive Order 11246 "Equal Employment Opportunity"
        The Voting Rights Act of 1965

1967   Executive Order 11375 "Gender Discrimination in the Federal Government"
        The Age Discrimination Employment Act of 1967 (ADEA)

1969   Executive Order 11478 "Discrimination in Federal Employment"
        Shapiro v. Thompson [394 U.S. 618 (1969)]

1970   The Postal Reorganization Act of 1970

1971   Executive Order 11590 "Postal Rate Commission"
        Aid to Families with Depended Children (AFDC)
        Wyman v. James [400 U.S. 309 (1971)]
        Griggs v. Duke Power Co. [401 U.S. 424 (1971)]

1972   The Equal Employment Act of 1972
        Reed v. Reed [404 U.S. 71 (1972)]
        Bradwell v. Illinois [83 U.S. 130 (1972)]

1973   The Rehabilitation Act of 1973
        San Antonio Independent School District v. Rodriguez
        [411 U.S. 1 (1973)]
        United States v. Virginia [411 U.S. 671 (1973)]
        Espinoza v. Farah Manufacturing Co., [414 U.S. 86
        (1973)]
        McDonnell Douglas Corporation v. Green [411 U.S.
        792 (1973)]

1974   Privacy Act
        Alexander v. Gardner-Denver Co., [415 U.S. 36
        (1974)]
        Cleveland Board of Education v. LaFLEUR [414 U.S.
        632 (1974)]
        Gedulbig v. Aiello [417 U.S. 484 (1974)]

1975   *Taylor v. Louisiana* [419 U.S. 522 (1975)]
        Johnson v. Railway Express Agency [421 U.S. 454
        (1975)]
        Albemarle Paper Co. V. Moody [422 U.S. 405 (1975)]
        Washington v. Davis [426 U.S. 229 (1975)]

1976   Race Discrimination Act of 1976
        Massachusetts Board of Retirement v. Murgia [427 U.S.
        307 (1967)]
        Craig v. Boren [429 U.S. 190 (1976)]
        Franks v. Bowman Transportation Co., [424 U.S. 747
        (1976)]

Washington v. Davis [426 U.S. 229 (1976)]

McDonald v. Santa Fe Trail Transportation Co., [427 U.S. 273 (1976)]

Massachusetts Board of Retirement v. Murgia [427 U.S. 307 (1976)]

Brown v. GSA [425 U.S. 820 (1976)]

Chandler v. Roudebush [425 U.S. 840 (1976)]

Hampton v. MOW SUN WONG [426 U.S. 88 (1976)]

1977   The Public Works Employment Act of 1977

Harriss v. Pan Am. World Airways, Inc., [74 F.R.D. 24, (1977)]

Teamsters v. United States [431 U.S. 324 (1977)]

United Airlines v. Evans [431 U.S. 553 (1977)]

Dothard v. Rawlinson [433 U.S. 321 (1977)]

Hazelwood School District v. U.S. [433 U.S. 299 (1977)]

Trans World Airlines Inc., v. Hardison [432 U.S. 63 (1977)]

United Airlines v. McHann [434 U.S. 193 (1977)]

1978   Executive Order 11246, as amended "Equal Employment Opportunity"
Executive Order 12106

Pregnancy Discrimination Act of 1978

Monell v. Department of Social Services [436 U.S. 658 (1978)]

University of California Rgents v. Bakke [438 U.S. 265 (1978)]

Furnco Construction Corporation v. Waters [438 U.S. 567 (1978)]

Board of Trustees v. Sweeney [58 Led. 2d 216 (1978)]

Foley v. Connelie [435 U.S. 291 (1978)]

Los Angeles Department of Water and Power v. Manhart [435 U.S. 702 (1978)]

1979   *Duren v. Missouri* [439 U.S. 357 (1979)]

        Orr v. Orr [99 S. Ct. 1102 (1979)]

        Southeastern Community College v. Davis [442 U.S. 397 (1979)]

        United Steelworkers of America v. Weber [61 Led 2.d 480 (1979)]

        New York City Transit Authority v. Beazer [59 Ed 2d 587 (1979)]

        Vance v. Bradley [59 L Ed 2d 171 (1979)]

        Ambach v. Norwick [60 L Ed 2d 49 (1979)]

        Oscar Mayer & Company v. Evans [60 LEd 2d 609 (1979)]

        Davis v. Passman [L.Ed. 2d. 846 (1979)]

        Givhan v. Western Line Consolidated School District [58 L. Ed. 2d 619 (1979)]

        Great American Federal Savings & Loan v. Novotny [60 L. Ed 2d 957 (1979)]

1980   *Garcia v. Gloor,* [618 F.2nd 264 (5th Cir. 1980)]

1981   Executive Order 11246

        Rostker v. Goldberg [453 U.S. 57 (1981)]

1982   *Mississippi University for Women v. Hogan* [458 U.S. 718 (1982)]

        Paxton v. Union Nat'l Bank, [688 F.2d 552 (1982)]

        Henson v. City of Dundee [682 F.2d 897 (llth Cir. 1982)]

1983   *Newport News Shipbuilding v. EEOC* [462 U.S. 669 (1983)]

1984   Sex Discrimination Act of 1984

        Hishon v. King & Spalding [104 S. Ct. 2229 (1984)]

        Grove City College v. Bell [104 S. Ct. 1211 (1984)]

Chevron U.S.A., Inc. v. Natural Resources Defense Council, Inc. [467 U.S. 837 (1984)]

1986   The Immigration Reform and Control Act (IRCA) of 1986
        Bowers v. Hardwick [478 U.S. 186 (1986)]
        Probe v. State Teachers' Retirement Sys., [780 F.2d 776, (1986)] *Cox. v. American Cast Iron Pipe Co.,* [784 F.2d 1546 (1986)]
        Meritor Savings Bank v. Vinson [477 U.S. 57 (1986)]

1987   *Johnson v. Transportation Agency of Santa Clara County, CA* [480 U.S. 616 (1987)]

1988   Age Discrimination Claims Assistance Act of 1988
        The Civil Rights Restoration Act of 1988
        United States v. Fausto [484 U.S. 439 (1988)]

1989   *Wards Cove Packing Co. v. Antonio* [490 v. 642 (1989)]
        Patterson v. McLean Credit Union [491 U.S. 164 (1989)]
        City of Richmond v. J. A. Croson Co. [488 U.S. 469 (1989)]
        Public Employees Retirement System of Ohio v. Betts [429 U.S. 159 (1989)]
        Webster v. Reproductive Health Services (1989)
        Price Waterhouse v. Hopkins [490 U.S. 228 (1989)]
        United Auto Workers v. Johnsons Controls, (1989)

1990   The Americans with Disability Act of 1990 (ADA)
        Missouri v. Jenkins [495 U.S. 33 (1990)]
        Spallone v. United States (1990)
        Older Workers Benefit Protection Act of 1990

1991   The Civil Rights Act of 1991
        Board of Education of Oklahoma City Public Schools v. Dowell [498 U.S. 237 (1991)]
        Chisom v. Roemer [112 L. Ed. 2nd 838 (1991)]

Gregory v. Ashcroft [501 U.S. 452 (1991)]

International Union, UAW v. Johnson Controls [499 U.S. 187 (1991)]

Pressley v. Etowah County Commission [112 S. Ct. 820 (1991)]

Gilmer v. Interstate/Johnson Lane Corp., [500 U.S. 20 (1991)]

Ellison v. Brady [924 F. 2d 872 (9th Cir. 1991)]

1992   Disability Discrimination Act of 1992

Freeman v. Pitts [503 U.S. 467 (1992)]

United States v. Fordice [505 U.S. 717 (1992)]

Planned Parenthood of Southeastern Pennsylvania v. Casey (1992)

1993   The Family and Medical Leave Act of 1993

The Religious Freedom Restoration Act (RFRA) of 1993

Harris v. Forklift Systems, Inc., [114 S. Ct. 367 (1993)]

St. Mary's Honor Center v. Hicks [509 U.S. 502 (1993)]

Shaw v. Reno [509 U.S. 630 (1993)]

Forbush v. J.C. Penney Co., [994 F.2d 1101, (1993)]

McDaniel v. Anheuser-Busch, Inc., [987 F.2d 298, 305 (1993)]

Burns v. McGregor Electronics Industries, Inc. (1993)

Garcia v. Spun Steak Co., [998 F.2d 1480, 1489 (9th Cir. 1993)]

Harris v. Forklift Systems Inc., [510 U.S. 17 (1993)]

1994   J.E.B. v. Alabama ex rel. T.B. [511 U.S. 127 (1994)]

1995   The Disability Discrimination Act of 1995 (DDA)

Executive Order 12968 "Access to classified information"

Adarand Constructors, Inc. v Pena [515 U.S. 2000 (1995)]

Miller v. Johnson [115 S. Ct. 2475 (1995)]

Board of Education of Pisscataway v. Taxman [96 U.S. 679]

Vernonia School District 47J v. Action [515 U.S. 646 (1995)]

Long v. First Union Corp., [894 F. Supp. 933, 941 (E.D. VA. 1995)]

Rhone-Poulenc Rorer, Inc., [51 F.3d 1293, 1302–03 (1995)]

1996   *Hopwood v. Texas 78* [U.S. 932 (1996)]

Shaw v. Hunt [(116 S. Ct. 1894 (1996)]

United States v. Virginia [518 U.S. 515 (1996)]

O'Connor v. Consolidated Coin Caterers Corp. [116 S. Ct. 1307 (1996)]

Romer v. Evans [517 U.S. 620, 632 (1996)]

Griffin v. Home Depot, Inc., [168 F.R.D. 187 (1996)]

Butler v. Home Depot, Inc., [C-94-4335 SL (1996)]

Shores v. Publix Super Markets, Inc., [95-1162-CIV-T-25(E), (1996]

EEOC v. Mason Tenders' District Counsel Welfare Fund (1996)

EEOC v. Monsanto Co. and Chevron Chemical Co. (1996)

EEOC v. General Dynamics Corp., (1996)

EEOC v. International Paper Company, (1996)

EEOC v. Southern California Edison Company, (1996)

1997   *Walters v. Metropolitan Educational Enterprises* [519 U.S. 202 (1997)]

Robinson v. Shell Oil Company [519 U.S. 337 (1997)]

General Electirc Co. v. Joiner (1997)

Gilday v. Mecosta County [96-1571 (6th Cir. 1997)]

Washington v. Glucksberg (1997)

Orlowski v. Dominick's Finer Foods, Inc., [172 F.R.D. 370 (1997)]

Eubanks v. Billington, [110 F.3d 87, 95 (1997)]
Matczak v. Frankford Candy and Chocolate Co., [97-1057(3rd Cir. 1997)]
Sutton v. United Air Lines [527 U.S. 471 (1997)]
Amchem Products, Inc. v. Windsor, [521 U.S. 591 (1997)]

1998   The Rehabilitation Act of 1973 as amended in 1998
Workforce Investment Act of 1998
Arnold v. United Parcel Services In.., [97-1781 (1998)]
Bragdon v. Abbott [118 S. Ct. 2196 (1998)]
Miller v. Albright (1998)
Oncale v. Sundowner Offshore Services, Inc. [523 U.S. 75 (1998)}
Allison v. Citgo Petroleum Corp [151 F.3d 402, 408 (1998)]
Wessman v. Gittens [160 F.3d 790 (1998)]
Faragher v. Boca Raton [524 U.S. 775 (1998)]
Burlington Indus. Inc., v. Ellerth [524 U.S. 742 (1998)]
Washington v. HCA Health Services of Texas Inc., [97-20310 (5th Cir. 1998)]
Faragher v. City of Boca Raton [524 U.s. 775 (1998)]

1999   Amendment to Executive Order 12958 "National Security Information"
Memo on Hiring People with Disabilities in the Federal Government issued by President Clinton
Memorandum on Annual Reports on Hate Crimes in Schools
Executive Order 13087 "Equal Employment Opportunity in the Federal Gov't"
EEOC v. Synchro-Start Prods. Inc., [29 F. Supp. 2d 911, 914-15 (ND. Ill. 1999)]
Roman v. Cornell Univ., [53 F. Supp. 2d 223, 237 (N.D. NY 1999)]
Sutton v. United Air Lines [527 U.S. 471 (1999)]

Otiz v. Fibreboard Corp., [119 S. Ct. 2295 (1999)]

2000   Executive Order on Nondiscrimination
Executive Order 13145 "Discrimination in Federal Employment based on genetic Information"
Executive Order 13153 "Equal Employment Opportunity in Federal Government"
Wynn & Wynn, P.C. v. Mass. Comm'n Against Discrimination, [431 Mass. 655 (2000)]
Willowbrook v. Olech [528 U.S. 562, 564 (2000)]
Apprendi v. New Jersey [530 U.S. 466, 499 (2000)]
Bush v. Gore [531 U.S. 98 (2000)]

2001   Executive Order 13224 "Executive Order on Terrorism Financing"
Executive Order "Community-Based Alternatives for Individuals with Disabilities"
Circuit City Stores v. Adams [532 U.S. 105 (2001)]
Clark County School District v. Breeden [532 U.S. 268 (2001)]
Board of Trustees of Univ. of Alabama v. Garrett [531 U.S. 356 (2001)]
NLRB v. Kentucky River Community Care, Inc., [532 U.S. 706 (2001)]
Nguyen v. INS, [533 U.S. 53 (2001)]
Alexander v. Sandoval [532 U.S. 275 (2001)]

2002   Executive Order 13252 "Exclusions from the Federal Labor-Management Relations Program"
Executive Order 13268 "Clarification of Certain Executive Orders Blocking Property and Prohibiting Certain Transactions"
Executive Order 13279 "Equal Protection of the Laws for Faith-Based and Community Organizations"
Executive Order 13282 "Further Adjustments of Certain Rates of Pay"

Toyota Motor Manufacturing, Kentucky Inc., v. Williams [534 U.S. 184 (2002)]

2003   Executive Order 13322 "Executive Order Adjustment to Rate Pay"
        Executive Order 12994 "Executive Act on Intellectual Disability"
        Desert Palace Inc., d/b/a Caesars Palace Hotel and Casino v. Costa [02 U.S. 679 (2003)]

2004   Executive Order "Further Executive Order Adjustment to Rate Pay"
        Executive Order 13360 "Providing Opportunities for Service-Disabled Veteran Businesses"
        Petrosino v. Bell Atlantic [385 F. 2d 210 (2004)]

2005   Amendments to Executive Order 12293 "The Foreign Service of the United States"
        Smith v. City of Jackson, [03-1160 U.S. (2005)]

Table 11: Landmark Judicial and Legislative Decisions
concerning Employment Discrimination

[Cases are listed in descending order according to the year the case was decided. Cases were selected considering their significance in employment discrimination on the basis of race, gender, religion, sex, national origin, disability and age, and impact in determining prima face cases, reasonable accommodation, hostile environment and Title VII cases.]

CASE	DECISION
Plessy v. Ferguson, 163 U.S. 537 (1896)	Racial Discrimination—Louisiana's segregate system is within constitutional boundaries: separate facilities for blacks and whites did not violate the 14th Amendment, as long as they were equal.
Brown v. Board of Education I, 347 U.S. 483 (1954)	Racial Discrimination—Recognized that segregation of children in public schools on basis of race is unconstitutional because it denies them equal opportunity and protection of laws under the 14th Amendment.
Brown v. Board of Education II, 347 U.S. 483 (1955)	Racial discrimination—It is the responsibility of the public schools to implement the principles which the Supreme Court supported in the first *Brown* case.

Griggs v. Duke Power Co., 401 U.S. 424 (1971)	Racial discrimination—Raised the question of good intent or absence of discriminatory intent: Duke's standardized testing requirement violated Title VII because they prevented African American employees from being hired or transferred to higher-paying departments within the company.
Reed v. Reed, 404 U.S. 71 (1972)	Sex Discrimination—Supreme court declared for the first time that sex discrimination violated the 14th Amendment.
Espinoza v. Farah Manufacturing Co., Inc., 414 U.S. 86 (1973)	National Origin Discrimination—The District Court granted petitioners' motion for summary judgment, but the Court of Appeals reversed, stating that "an employer's refusal to hire a person because he is not a United States citizen does not constitute employment discrimination on the basis of 'national origin' requirements."
Taylor v. Louisiana, 419 U.S. 522 (1975)	Supreme Court supported women's rights.
Rostker v. Goldberg, 453 U.S. 57 (1981)	Gender Discrimination—The "male only" military draft registration did not violate the Due Process Clause of the 5th Amendment.

Mississippi University for Women v. Hogan, 458 U.S. 718 (1982)	<u>Gender Discrimination</u>—The state statute prevented men from enrolling in MUW violated the Equal Protection Clause of the Fourteenth Amendment: The Court held that "the state did not provide an 'exceedingly persuasive justification' for the gender-based distinction."
Bowers v. Hardwick, 478 U.S. 186 (1986)	<u>Sexual Orientation Discrimination</u>— There is no constitutional protection for homosexuals to engage in consensual sodomy, thus the state could determine these actions as illegal.
Wards Cove Packing Co. v. Antonio, 490 U.S. 642 (1989)	<u>Disparate Impact Claims</u>—The claims were rejected by the District Court for failure of proof.
Gregory v. Ashcroft, 501 U.S. 452 (1991)	<u>Age Discrimination</u>—Missouri's mandatory retirement requirement for its state court judges did not violate the 1967 federal Age Discrimination in Employment Act (ADEA) and the Fourteenth Amendment's Equal Protection Clause.
Shaw v. Reno, 509 U.S. 630 (1993)	<u>Racial Discrimination</u>—Burden of proof requirement: evidence of intentional discrimination; the North Carolina residents' claim, "that the State created a racially gerrymandered district," did raise a valid constitutional issue under the 14th Amendment's Equal Protection Clause.

J.E.B. v. Alabama ex rel T.B., 511 U.S. 127 (1994)	Sex Discrimination—Excluding jurors on the basis of gender is a violation of the equal protection clause of the Fourteenth Amendment.
Romer v. Evans, 517 U.S. 620, 632 (1996)	Sexual Orientation Discrimination—Colorado's State Constitution, "forbidding the extension of official protections to those who suffer discrimination due to their sexual orientation," violate the Fourteenth Amendment's Equal Protection Clause.
Shaw v. Hunt, 116 S. Ct. 1894 (1996)	Racial Discrimination—North Carolina's redistricting plan constituted racial gerrymandering in violation of the Fourteenth Amendment's Equal Protection Clause.
United States v. Virginia, 518 U.S. 515 (1996)	Sex Discrimination—Virginia's "single sex institutions" admissions policy violated the Fourteenth Amendment's Equal Protection Clause.
Robinson v. Shell Oil Company, 519 U.S. 337 (1997)	Employment Discrimination—The Court held that Title VII's ban of employment discrimination applied to both past and present employees
Oncale v. Sundowner Offshore Services, Inc. (1998)	Sex Discrimination—Does sex discrimination apply to same-sex sexual harassment? The Court held that Title VII prohibits all forms of discrimination, regardless of the victim's gender.

Sutton v. United Air Lines, 97 U.S. 1943 (1999)	<u>Disability Discrimination</u>—The Court held that the determination of disability under 42 U.S.C. Section 12102(2)(A) should be made "in reference to an individual's ability to mitigate his or her impairment through corrective measures."
Apprendi v. New Jersey, 530 U.S. 466, 499 (2000)	<u>Reasonable Doubt</u>—The Court held that "the Due Process Clause requires that any fact that increases the penalty for a crime beyond the prescribed statutory maximum, other than the fact of a prior conviction, must be submitted to a jury and proved beyond a reasonable doubt."
Desert Palace Inc., d/b/a Caesars Palace Hotel and Casino v. Costa, 02 U.S. 679 (2003)	<u>Direct Discrimination</u>—Direct evidence of discrimination is not required to obtain a mixed-motive instruction under Title VII of the Civil Rights Act of 1964 as amended by the Civil Rights Act of 1991.
Smith v. City of Jackson, [03-1160 U.S. (2005)	<u>Disparate Impact Discrimination</u>— The Court held that "Disparate impact claim—a claim alleging unintentional discrimination – can be made under the Age Discrimination in Employment Act of 1967" however, the petitioners did not provide valid claims.

LAW	DISCRIPTION
Civil Rights Act of 1866	Gave African Americans the right to sell and buy property the same as whites.
Civil Rights Act of 1875	Involved political and social equality, however the Supreme Court voided it.
Executive Order 10925 of 1961	"Establishing the President's Committee on EEO" -issued by President Kennedy to protect minority's rights
Civil Rights Act of 1964	Banned discrimination based on race, color, sex, religion, national origin.
Executive Order 11246 of 1965	"Equal Employment Opportunity"—issued by Johnson and EEO's transferred to the Civil Service Commission.
The Voting Rights Act of 1965	Reflects Congress's intention to free US from racial discrimination
Executive Order 11375 of 1967	"Gender Discrimination in the Federal Government"-issued by President Johnson to prohibit discrimination, including sex discrimination.
The Age Discrimination Employment Act of 1967	ADEA promotes employment based on ability rather than age.
The Equal Employment Act of 1972	Further expanded Title VII
The Rehabilitation Act of 1973	Protects persons in workplace, who have physical or mental impairments.
Race Discrimination Act of 1976	Prohibits unlawful treatment on the basis of race.

Executive Order 11246 of 1978	"Equal Employment Opportunity"—issued by President Johnson and contracting-agency enforcement personnel were reassigned to the Labor Department.
Executive Order 11246 of 1981	As amended—issued by President Jimmy Carter, creation of OFCC within the Labor Department.
Age Discrimination Claims Assistance Act of 1988	Restored the rights of workers to seek redress due to EEOC delays in processing of claims.
Older Workers Benefit Protection Act of 1990	Congress prohibits discrimination against older workers.
The Civil Rights Act of 1991	Further amended Title VII of the Civil Rights Act of 1964.
The Disability Discrimination Act of 1995 (DDA)	Prohibits discrimination on the basis of disability.
Amendment to Executive Order 12958 in 1999	"National Security Information"—enforced by President William J. Clinton
Executive Order 13087 of 1999	"Equal Employment Opportunity in the Federal Government"—issued by President Clinton, further Amendment to Executive Order 11478.
Executive Order on Nondiscrimination of 2000	issued by President William J. Clinton.
Executive Order 13145 of 2000	"Discrimination in Federal Employment based on genetic information"—issued by President William J. Clinton.

Executive Order 13153 of 2000	"Equal Employment Opportunity in Federal Government"—further amended Executive Order 11478.
Executive Order 13224 0f 2001	"Executive Order on Terrorism Financing"—issued by Bush, block assets of certain entities to prevent terrorism acts.
Executive Order of 2001	"Community-Based Alternatives for Individuals with Disabilities"—issued by President Bush.
Executive Order 13252 of 2002	"Exclusions from the Federal Labor-Management Relations Program."
Executive Order 13279 of 2002	"Equal Protection of the Laws for Faith-Based and Community Organizations."
Executive Order 13282 of 2002	"Further Adjustments of Certain Rates of Pay."
Executive Order 13322 of 2003	"Executive Order Adjustment to Rate Pay."
Executive Order of 2004	"Further Executive Order Adjustment to Rate Pay"—issued by President Bush.
Amendments to Executive Order 12293 in 2005	"The Foreign Service of the United States"—established the following salary classes with titles for the Senior Foreign Service.

APPENDIX

Table 12: Resident Population Estimates of the Unites States By Gender, Race, and Income Status: April 1, 1992 to April 1, 2004

U.S. RESIDENT POPULATION

Year	Total Population	Male	Female	White	African-American	American-Indian	Hispanic/Latino	Asian
1992	255,030	124,424	130,606	212,874	31,683	2,149	24,283	8,324
1993	257,783	125800	131983	214691	32195	2187	2522	8710
1994	260,289	127076	133266	216379	32672	2222	26160	9054
1995	262,803	128,293	134,510	218,023	33,116	2,256	27,107	9,408
1996	265,229	129504	135724	219636	33537	2290	28099	9765
1997	267,784	130783	137001	221333	33989	2326	29182	10135
1998	270,248	132030	138218	222980	34427	2361	30252	10479
1999	272,691	133,277	139,414	224,611	34,862	2,397	31,337	10,820
2000	281,422	138,054	143,368	228,610	35,810	2,673	35,650	10,243
2001	285102	140009	145085	230502	36247	2711	37062	11105
2002	282,100	95,386	99,436	194,822	34,676	2945	37,438	12,201
2003	290,810	143,037	147,773	234,196	37,099	2,787	39,899	11,925
2004	294,492	138,054	143,068	211,461	34,658	2,476	35,306	10,243
Total 92-04	3,554,783	1,731,874	1,806,457	2,655,296	410,295	28,835	346,859	120,211

Change of Income Status, 1992–2004

Number with Earnings Households By Total Money Income

Year	Male	Female	White	Black	Hispanic	Asian
1992	48551	33241	75107	11269	7153	2262
1993	49818	33524	75697	11281	7362	2233
1994	51580	34155	77004	11655	7735	2040
1995	52667	35482	76932	11577	7939	2777
1996	53787	36430	77240	12109	8225	2998
1997	54909	37683	77936	12474	8590	3125
1998	56951	38785	78577	12579	9060	3308
1999	58299	40871	79819	12838	9579	3742
2000	59602	41719	80527	13174	10034	3963
2001	58712	41369	80818	13315	10499	4071
2002	58761	41876	81166	13465	11,339	3917
2003	58772	41908	81148	13629	11,693	4040

Source: Population Estimates Program, Population Division, U.S. Census Bureau, Washington, D.C. April 1, 1990 to July 1, 1999.

Source: U.S. Census Bureau, Statistical Abstract of the United States: 2004–2005 (Numbers in thousands. 226,546 represents 226,546,000. Consistent with the 1980–2004 population estimates base.)

Table 13: Resident Population Estimates of the Unites States by Discrimination Type: April 1, 1992 to April 1, 2004

Source: Office of Research, Information, and Planning from EEOC's Charge Data Summary Report FY 1992—FY 2004.

EEOC TRENDS OF EMPLOYMENT DISCRIMINATION BY TYPE						
	Age		*Disability*		*National Origin*	
Year	Receipts	Resolutions	Receipts	Resolutions	Receipts	Resolutions
1992	19,573	19,975	1,048	88	7,434	7,196
1993	19,809	19,761	15,274	4,502	7,454	6,788
1994	19,618	13,942	18,859	12,523	7,414	6,453
1995	17,416	17,033	19,798	18,900	7,035	7,619
1996	15,719	17,699	18,046	23,451	6,687	9,047
1997	15,785	18,279	18,108	24,200	6,712	8,795
1998	15,191	15,995	17,806	23,324	6,778	8,482
1999	14,141	15,448	17,007	22,152	7,108	8,750
2000	16,008	14,672	15,864	20,475	7,792	8,691
2001	17,405	15,155	16,470	19,084	8,025	8,899
2002	19,921	18,673	15,964	18,804	9,046	9,952
2003	19,124	17,352	15,377	16,915	8,450	9,172
2004	17,837	15,792	15,376	16,949	8,361	8,943
Total 92-04	227,547	219776	204,997	221,367	98,296	108,787

EEOC TRENDS OF EMPLOYMENT DISCRIMINATION continued…

Sex Discrimination

Year	Gender		Pregnancy		Equal Pay	
	Receipts	Resolutions	Receipts	Resolutions	Receipts	Resolutions
1992	21,796	20,102	3,385	3,045	1,294	1,185
1993	23,919	21,606	3,577	3,145	1,328	1,120
1994	25,860	21,545	4,170	3,181	1,381	1,171
1995	26,181	26,726	4,191	3,908	1,275	1,249
1996	23,813	30,965	3,743	4,186	969	1,235
1997	24,728	32,836	3,977	4,595	1,134	1,172
1998	24,454	31,818	4,219	4,467	1,071	1,134
1999	23,907	30,643	4,166	4,343	1,044	1,026
2000	25,194	29,631	4,160	4,480	1,270	1,235
2001	25,140	28,602	4,287	4,280	1,251	1,158
2002	25,536	29,088	4,714	4,778	1,256	1,182
2003	24,362	27,146	4,649	4,847	1,167	1,071
2004	24,249	26,598	4,512	4,512	1,011	996
Total 92-04	319,139	357,306	53,750	53,767	15,451	14934

EEOC TRENDS OF EMPLOYMENT
DISCRIMINATION continued....

Year	Sexual Harassment		Race		Religion	
	Receipts	Resolutions	Receipts	Resolutions	Receipts	Resolutions
1992	10,532	7,484	29,548	28,497	1,388	1,297
1993	11,908	9,971	31,695	27,440	1,449	1,286
1994	14,420	11,478	31,656	25,253	1,546	1,274
1995	15,549	13,802	29,986	31,674	1,581	1,606
1996	15,342	15,861	26,287	35,127	1,564	1,911
1997	15,889	17,333	29,199	36,419	1,709	2,137
1998	15,618	17,115	28,820	35,716	1,786	2,247
1999	15,222	16,524	28,819	35,094	1,811	2,187
2000	15,836	16,726	28,945	33,188	1,939	2,230
2001	15,475	16,383	28,912	32,077	2,127	2,217
2002	14,396	15,792	29,910	33,199	2,572	2,729
2003	13,566	14,534	28,526	30,702	2,532	2,690
2004	13,136	13,786	27,696	29,631	2,466	2,676
Total 92-04	186,889	186,789	379,999	414,017	24,470	26,487

BIBLIOGRAPHY

Adarand Constructors, Inc. v Pena [515 U.S. 2000 (1995)]

Americans with Disability Act of 1990, Title I & Title V, § 501. (Pub. L. 101-336).

Age Discrimination In Employment Act of 1967. (Pub. L. 90-202).

Anderson, Bernard, E. (1996). The Ebb and Flow of Enforcing Executive Order 11246. The American Economic Review. 86(2), 298-301.

Arnold v. United Parcel Services Inc., [97-1781 (1998)]

Bamforth, Nicholas. (1993). The Changing Concept of Sex Discrimination. *The Modern Law Review.* 56(6), 872-880.

Bawden, Lee, D., & Skidmore, Felicity. (1989). *Rethinking Employment Policy.* Washington, D.C.: The Urban Institute Press.

Bradfor, Sharon, T. (1990). Relief for Hostile Work Environment Discrimination: Restoring Title VII's Remedial Powers. *The Yale Law Journal,* 99(7), 1611-1630.

Bryner, Gary. (1981). Congress, Courts and Agencies: Equal Employment and Limits of Policy

Implementation. *Political Science Quarterly*, 96(3), 411-430.

Bureau of the Census, U.S. Dep't of Comm., (1983). *America Black Population 1970*-1982.

Burstein, Paul. (1998). *Discrimination, Jobs and Politics: The Struggle for Equal Employment Opportunity in the United States since the New Deal.* Chicago, IL: The University of Chicago Press.

Chambers, Julius, L. & Goldstein, Barry. (1986). Title VII: The Continuing Challenge of Establishing Fair Employment Practices. *Law and Contemporary Problems.* 49(4), 9-23.

Chevron U.S.A., Inc. v. Natural Resources Defense Council, Inc. [467 U.S. 837 (1984)]

Chicago Tribune (Sept. 2000). *Immigrant Labor Force in U.S. Up Sharply.* 2000 WL 3704780**.**

Civil Rights Act of 1866. (42 USC 1981).

Civil Rights Act of 1964. Title VII. Section 703 (a) (2).

Cruz, Amaury, (1995). *English Only? For Employees That is the Question.* Retrieved from www. lexarian.com.

Congressman Mark Kennedy. (Interview, May 04, 2005). *Congressman Kennedy's view on Employment Discrimination.* Washington D.C.: Longworth House Office Building.

Dean, John, P. (1983). Congressional Power Under Section Five of the Fourteenth Amendment. *Columbia Law Review.* 78, 372-408.

Deitch, Cynthia. (1993). Gender, Race, and Class Politics and the Inclusion of Women in the

Title VII of the 1964 Civil Rights Act. *Gender and Society.* 7(2), 183-203.

Desert Palace Inc., d/b/a Caesars Palace Hotel and Casino v. Costa [02 U.S. 679 (2003)]

Doyle, Brian. (1997). Enabling Legislation or Dissembling Law? The Disability Discrimination Act 1995. *The Modern Law Review.* 60(1), 64-78.

EEOC v. Synchro-Start Prods. Inc., [29 F. Supp. 2d 911, 914-15 (ND. Ill. 1999)]

Eisaguierre, Lynne. (1999). *Affirmative Action: A Reference Handbook.* Santa Barbara, CA: ABC-CLIO, Inc.

Equal Employment Opportunity Commission, (2005). *Age Discrimination in Employment Act (ADEA) Charges FY 1992-FY 2004.* Retrieved from *http://www.eeoc.gov/stats/adea.html.*

Equal Employment Opportunity Commission, (2005). *Equal Pay Charges FY 1992—FY 2004.* Retrieved from http://www.eeoc.gov/stats/epa.html.

Equal Employment Opportunity Commission, (2005). *National Origin-*Charges *FY 1992-FY 2004.* Retrieved from http://www.eeoc.gov/stats/origin.html.

Equal Employment Opportunity Commission, (2005). *Pregnancy Discrimination Charges EEOC & FEPAs Combined: FY 1992—FY 2004.* Retrieved from http://www.eeoc.gov/stats/pregnanc.html.

Equal Employment Opportunity Commission, (2005). *Race-Based Charges FY 1992-FY 2004.*

Retrieved from http://www.eeoc.gov/stats/race. html.

Equal Employment Opportunity Commission, (2005). *Religion-Based Charges FY 1992-FY 2004.* Retrieved from http://www.eeoc.gov/ stats/religion.html.

Equal Employment Opportunity Commission, (2005). *Sex-Based Charges FY 1992-FY 2004.* Retrieved from http://www.eeoc.gov/stats/sex. html.

Equal Employment Opportunity Commission, (2005). *Sexual Harassment Charges EEOC & FEPAs Combined: FY 1992-FY 2004.* Retrieved from http://www.eeoc.gov/stats/harass.html.

Equal Employment Opportunity Commission, (2004). *Americans with Disability Act of 1990 Charges (ADA).* Retrieved from http://www. eeoc.gov/stats/ada.html.

Equal Employment Opportunity Commission, (2002). *National Origin Discrimination.*

EEOC Compliance Manual: Section 13. Retrieved from http://www.eeoc.gov/policy/docs/ national-origin.html#N_10_.

Equal Employment Opportunity Commission, (2000). *Job Patterns for Minorities and Women in Private Industry.* Retrieved from http://www. eeoc.gov/stats/jobpat/2000/index.html.

Equal Employment Opportunity Commission, (1998). *Definitions of Terms.* Retrieved from http://www.eeoc.gov/stats/define.html.

Equal Pay Act of 1963. (Pub. L. 88–38).

Fair Labor Standards Act of 1938.

Fuentes, Sonia, Pressman. (1972). The Law against Sex Discrimination in Employment and its Relationship to Statistics. *The American Statistician.* 26(2), 16–21.

Garcia v. Gloor, [618 F.2nd 264 (5th Cir. 1980)]

Garcia v. Spun Steak Co., [998 F.2d 1480, 1489 (9th Cir. 1993)]

Gilday v. Mecosta County [96-1571 (6th Cir. 1997)]

Graham, Hugh, Davis. (1992). The Origin of Affirmative Action: Civil Rights and the Regulatory State. *Annals of the American Academy of Political and Social Science.* 523, 50–62.

Griggs v. Duke Power Co. [401 U.S. 424 (1971)]

Guy, Mary, E. (2003). The Difference that Gender Makes. In Hays, Steven, W. *Public Personnel Administration: Problems and Prospects* (4th ed.).(pp. 256–270). Upper Saddle River, NJ: Prentice Hall.

Harris v. Forklift Systems Inc., [510 U.S. 17 (1993)]

Hays, Steven, W. (2003). *Public Personnel Administration: Problems and Prospects* (4th ed.). Upper Saddle River, NJ: Prentice Hall.

Hellriegel, Don & Short, Larry Short. (1972). Equal Employment Opportunity in the Federal Government. *Public Administration Review*, 32, 851–858.

Henson v. City of Dundee [682 F.2d 897 (llth Cir. 1982)]

International Union, UAW v. Johnson Controls [499 U.S. 187 (1991)]

Jones, Timothy, L. (1993). *American with Disabilities Act: A Review of Best Practices.* New York, NY: American Management Association.

Kellough, J. Edward. (2003a). Equal Employment Opportunity and Affirmative Action in the Public Sector. In Hays, Steven, W. *Public Personnel Administration: Problems and Prospects* (4th ed.). (pp. 209–224). Upper Saddle River, NJ: Prentice Hall.

Kellough, J. Edward. (1992b). Affirmative Action in Government Employment. *Annals* of the American Academy of Political and Social Science. 523, 117–130.

Long, Robert, Emmett. (1996). The Reference Shell: *Affirmative Action.* New York, NY: The H. W. Wilson Company.

Long v. First Union Corp., [894 F. Supp. 933, 941 (E.D. VA. 1995)]

Manni, Bonnie, G. (2003). Disabled or Not Disabled: How Does the Americans With Disabilities Act Effect Employment Policies? In Hays, Steven, W. *Public Personnel Administration: Problems and Prospects* (4th ed.). (pp. 271–286). Upper Saddle River, NJ: Prentice Hall.

Maschke, Karen, J. (1989). *Litigation, Courts, and Women Workers.* New York, NY: Praeger Publishers.

Matczak v. Frankford Candy and Chocolate Co., [97-1057(3rd Cir. 1997)]

Morris, Andrew, J. (1995). On the Normative Foundations of Indirect Discrimination Law: Understanding the Competing Models of Discrimination Law as Aristotelian Forms of Justice. *Oxford Journal of Legal Studies,* Vol., 15(2), 199–228.

Older Workers Benefit Protection Act. (Pub. L. 101-433).

Personnel Policy Inc. Service Inc. (Feb., 2004). *English-only Policies and the melting pot.* Retrieved on May 10, 2005 from http://employmentblawg. blogspot.com/

Player, Mack, A. (1988). *Employment Discrimination Law.* St. Paul, MN: West Publishing Company.

Player, Mack, A. (1992). *Federal Law of Employment Discrimination in a Nutshell* (3rd ed.). St. Paul, MN: West Publishing Company.

Price Waterhouse v. Hopkins [490 U.S. 228 (1989)]

Pynes, Joan, E. (2004a). *Human Resources Management for Public and Nonprofit Organizations.* San Francisco, CA: Jossey-Bass A Wiley Imprint.

Pynes, Joan, E. (2004b). Equal Employment Opportunity. In *Human Resources Management for Public and Nonprofit Organizations* (pp. 72–93). San Francisco, CA: Jossey-Bass A Wiley Imprint.

Pynes, Joan, E. (2004c). Valuing a Diverse Workforce. In *Human Resources Management for Public and Nonprofit Organizations* (pp. 94–120). San Francisco, CA: Jossey-Bass A Wiley Imprint.

Rehabilitation Act of 1973.

Roberts, Robert. N. (1985). The Public Law Litigation Model and "Memphis v. Scotts". *Public Administration Review.* 45(4), 527-532.

Roman v. Cornell Univ., [53 F. Supp. 2d 223, 237 (N.D. NY 1999)]

Rosenthal, Albert. (1973). Employment Discrimination and Law. *Annals of the American Academy of Political and Social Science.* 407, 91–101.

Rutherglen, George. (1995). Discrimination an its Discontent. *Virginia Law Review.* 81(1). 117–147.

Seldon, Sally, Coleman. (2003). Sexual Harassment in the Workplace. In Hays, Steven, W. *Public Personnel Administration: Problems and Prospects* (4th ed.). (pp. 225–237). Upper Saddle River, NJ: Prentice Hall.

Smith, Arthur, B. Jr. (1980). The Law and Equal Employment Opportunity: What's Past Should Not Be Prologue. *Industrial and Labor Relations Review,* 33(4), 493–505.

Smith v. City of Jackson, [03-1160 U.S. (2005)]

Spognardi, Mark, A. (2003). *Supreme Court Opens Gates to Plaintiff "Mixed-Motive" Employment Discrimination Lawsuits.* Chicago, IL: Holland & Knight LLP. Retrieved from http://www.hklaw.com/Publications/OtherPublication.asp?ArticleID=2270.

Steel, George, W. and Guss, Michael, J. (2005). *Employment Law.* Harvey Cruse, P.C. Retrieved from http://www.harveykruse.com/employme.htm.

Stephan-Goetz Richter & Daniel Bachman, (1999). How to Keep Growth Alive: Welcome More Immigrants. *Wall St. Journal.*1999 WL-WSJ.

Stockdale, Margaret, S. (1996). *Sexual Harassment in the Workplace: Perspectives, Frontiers, and Response Strategies* (5th ed.). Thousand Oaks, CA: Sage Publications.

Sutton v. United Airlines Inc., [97 U.S. 1943 (1999)]

Title VII of the Civil Rights Act of 1964, 42 § 2000 (e). (Pub. L. 88-352).

The Civil Rights Act of 1991, 902 § 1977. (Pub. L. 102-166).

Twomey, David, P. (1994). *Equal Employment Opportunity Law* (3rd ed.). Cincinnati, OH: South-Western Publishing Co.

United Auto Workers v. Johnsons Controls, (1989)

U.S. Census Bureau publications: 1990 Census of Population: "Social and Economic Characteristics, Nativity, Citizenship, Year of Entry, and Language Spoken at Home." Retrieved from http://www.census.gov/prod/cen1990/cp2/cp-2-1.pdf.

U.S. Census Bureau publications: 2000 Census of Population: "Age by Language Spoken at Home by Ability to Speak English for the Population 5 Years and Over." Retrieved from http://factfinder.census.gov/servlet/DTTable?ds_name=D&geo_id=D&mt_name=ACS_C2SS_EST_G2000_P035&_lang=en.

U.S., Civil Service Commission, (1965). *Study of Minority Group Employment in the Federal Government,* Washington, D.C.: Government Printing Office.

U.S., Civil Service Commission, (1970). *Study of Minority Group Employment in the Federal Government,* Office of Personnel Management, Equal Employment Opportunity Statistics.

U.S., Civil Service Commission, (1980). *Study of Minority Group Employment in the Federal Government,* Office of Personnel Management, Equal Employment Opportunity Statistics.

U.S., Civil Service Commission, (1990). *Study of Minority Group Employment in the Federal Government,* Affirmative Employment Statistics.

U.S. Congress. House. Subcommittee on the Civil Service of the Committee on Government Reform. *EEO Data and Complaint Processing Problems.* 106th Cong., 2nd sess., 2000.

U.S. Congress. Joint Economic Committee. *Hearings on Economic Problems of Women.* 93rd Cong., 1st sess., 1973.

U.S. Congress. *Legislative History of the Equal Employment Opportunity Act of 1972, Amending Title VII of the Civil Rights Act of 1964.* Prepared by the Subcommittee on Labor of the Committee on Labor and Public Welfare.

U.S. EEOC. *Legislative History of Title VII and XI of Civil Rights Act of 1964.* Washington D.C.: GAO.

U.S. Congress. Senate. Subcommittee on Constitutional Rights of the Senate Committee on the Judiciary. *Hearings on Civil Rights Act of 1967.* 90th Cong., 1st sess., 1965.

U.S. Congress. Senate. Committee on Labor and Human Resources. *Hearings on the Equal Employment Opportunity Commission.* 98th Cong., 1st sess., 1983.

U.S. Federal Code, 42 § 12116.

U.S. Federal Code, 42, § 2000 (e) (2).

U.S. Federal Code, 42, § 2000 (e) (3).

U.S. Federal Code § 2000 (e) (k).

U.S. Federal Code § 12101.

U.S. Federal Code, 29, § 2601.

U.S. Federal Code, 29 § 215

U.S. Federal Code, 29 § 255.

U.S. Federal Code, 29, § 621.

U.S. Federal Code, 29, § 206 (d) (1).

U.S., *Federal Register,* 27 June 1941, p. 3109.

U.S. *Federal Register,* 13 Nov. 1940, p. 4445–48.

Wards Cove Packing Co. v. Antonio [490 v. 642 (1989)]

Washington v. Davis [426 U.S. 229 (1975)]

Washington v. HCA Health Services of Texas Inc., [97-20310 (5th Cir. 1998)]

Weinberg, Gerhard, L. (1996). Changes in the Place of Women in the Historical Profession: A personal Perspective. *The History Teacher.* 29(3), 323-327.

Weizer, Paul, I. (2000). *The Supreme Court and Sexual Harassment: Preventing Harassment while*

Preserving Free Speech Lanham, MD: Lexington Books.

White, Rebecca, Hanner. (2000). Deference and Disability Discrimination. *Michigan Law Review.* 99(3), 532-587.

Volokh, Eugine (1997). What Speech Does "Hostile Environment" Harassment Law Restrict? *Geo. Law Journal.* 85(627),1871-72.

ABOUT THE AUTHOR

Dr. Ermira Babamusta is a former Obama Administration presidential campaign director. Prior to her leadership position for President Obama, Dr. Babamusta began her career in foreign affairs at the U.S. Congress with Senator Tom Harkin and Congressman Mark Kennedy in Washington DC, followed by her work at the Peace-keeping department at United Nations Headquarters in New York. She is the founder of the two-year initiative "Peace Action Foundation" in support of U.S. military and veterans.

Ermira graduated with a Ph.D. in Political Science and holds two MA degrees in Political Science and Public Administration. She completed the UN Diplomacy graduate program and Harvard's "National Defense & Security" mastery program. Her Strasbourg study abroad program was in European Union Law and Institutions in France.

Dr. Ermira Babamusta is the recipient of numerous awards and honors, in recognition of her professional achievements, leadership in politics, and community building, namely: The White House President's Award by President Obama, Distinguished Humanitarian Award by US Congress, House Majority Leader Harry Reid, Inaugural 10 Under 10 Award, Woman of the Year, Woman of Courage Award, Excellence in Leadership Award, etc.

Ermira Babamusta is the author of "*Political Trust in Kosovo: Exploring Cultural and Institutional Dynamics*," "*The Legislative Journey of Employment Discrimination*," and "*Diplomacy and Nation Building in Kosovo*."